Corporate Sabaki

The strategy for attacking your opponent's blind spot to grow your business

By John Roberts

First produced and copywritten in 2024 by Florir Ltd
(NZBN9429041571279) on behalf of
John Charles Roberts
54 Hobill Avenue, Wiri, Manukau, 2104, Auckland, New Zealand.

Typeset in Calibri Regular 11pt

©All rights reserved – John Charles Roberts 2024

The moral rights of the author have been asserted.

Cover design by Florir Ltd
Cover image: ©Florir Ltd
Imagery throughout the book: From the personal archives of John Roberts - © - All rights reserved

Corporate Sabaki™ is a trademark owned by Florir Ltd on behalf of John Roberts. This trademark is used throughout this book.

Disclaimer:

The material in this publication is of the nature of general comment only and does not represent professional advice. It is not intended to provide specific guidance for any particular circumstances and it should not be solely relied on as the basis for any decision as your own due diligence is required. Readers should obtain professional advice where appropriate. To the maximum extent permitted by law, the author and publisher disclaim all responsibility and liability to any person, arising directly or indirectly from any person taking or not taking action based on the information in this publication.

Contents

Chapters

Corporate Sabaki...1

Contents..3

Acknowledgements...5

Preface: How my martial arts experience helped create this concept 7

Introduction: The Intersection of Martial Arts and Business Strategy...9

Understanding Sabaki: The Core Principles 18

From Dojo to Boardroom: Translating Martial Arts into Business Tactics..24

The Philosophy of Movement: Navigating Business Challenges...30

Reading the Opponent: Market Analysis and Competitor Insight 39

Strategic Positioning: Finding the Right Stance in Business 46

Timing and Distance: The Art of Strategic Decision Making 53

Redirecting Energy: Turning Challenges into Opportunities 63

Anticipation and Adaptation: Staying Ahead in a Competitive Market..71

Counter-Strategy: Defending Against Competitor Moves80

Controlled Aggression: Knowing When to Strike in Business 90

Finding the Opening: Identifying and Exploiting Market Gaps 99

Balance and Stability: Maintaining a Strong Business Foundation 108

Continuous Learning: The Role of Training and Development 118

Resilience and Recovery: Bouncing Back from Setbacks 126

Building a Team: Leveraging Collective Strengths 134

The Power of Perception and Reputation: Shaping Your Image 145

Ethical Strategy: Winning with Integrity 154

Fluidity and Flow: Use Their Strength to Your Advantage 164

Conclusion: The Sabaki Way in Business and Beyond 172

Acknowledgements

I just want to take this opportunity to thank my wife Courtney, you are my rock and so incredibly understanding with all of my creative pursuits and businesses. I am a better person for having you in my life and I will continue doing what I can to build a better life for us and our boys.

To my sons Liam and Ollie, you are my driving force. Everything that I do in my life is to make your lives easier and so that I can spend more time living a life that I love with you.

To mum and dad, thank you for your kindness and support with everything that you do for our family. Also thank you mum for your support and help with this book, I am forever grateful for your guidance and that your brain is like a dictionary.

To Kate, thank you for having a big part in the proofing of this book and refining some of my well entrenched habits; along with your insight on areas that I could bring some more creativity to. Thank you also for always being a good sparring partner to practice sabaki in real life.

To Donna, thank you for helping to look after Courtney and my boys so that I could spend time creating this book. I appreciate you.

To family and friends, If I mentioned everyone that has had an impact directly on my that lead to producing this book my word count would be doubled. You are all so amazing and I appreciate the support that you give to myself and to my family.

To Kevin D'Ambrose Smith, A huge thank you for being a constant creative source towards the growth of my businesses, I am lucky to have you as a mentor and I appreciate all of your advice and guidance.

To Shihan Mark Stewart, I am forever thankful that I had the experience of being part of your dojo and community; I appreciate the support and guidance that you have given me over the years and for being such a strong figure through my early life. I wouldn't have the concept of this book without your lessons over the many years.

To Jack Arbuckle, for suggesting that I actually write a book. I appreciate your support and belief in my knowledge and methodologies.

To anyone that I have missed directly I want to thank you for your part in this journey.

Osu.

Preface: How my martial arts experience helped create this concept

I first started karate at age 10 after being bullied at primary school in Auckland, New Zealand; bullying is such a horrible thing for kids and adults to go through. My experience included having to bring 2 lunches to school each day just so that I would be able to eat. I was lucky as the bullying that I experienced was all just intimidation tactics and didn't turn physical as I was a fast runner and also being a smaller kid was quite good at what I would now call stealth manoeuvres.

As my mum was looking for dojos around from us, she drove past one that was down the road from a local second-hand shop. This dojo was an Ashihara Kaikan karate dojo run by Shihan Mark Stewart. At this dojo I learned the essence of sabaki and how to implement it in a fighting situation. I also learned the basics of defending myself and building self-confidence both of which are positive outcomes gained by students of martial arts. As soon as I joined this dojo the bullying stopped and I was never bullied again due to others knowing that I knew how to fight. I was also incredibly lucky when I was 15 years old, I along with a few other students had the opportunity to go to Japan to have a couple of weeks training at different Ashihara dojos including Honbu (headquarters) in Matsuyama which was an amazing experience. The picture below is of one training session at the Ashihara Kaikan Honbu.
Circled is myself as a little 15-year-old karate student learning from some true masters.

Training at Honbu was an amazing experience where I got to experience a class run by Hidenori Ashihara himself and was star struck the entire time. Through these training sessions I was able to refine my sabaki technique and slowly continue towards mastery myself (which will always be a continuing journey).

When I completed my schooling, I moved into the business world working in our family business sweeping floors and stocking shelves in the warehouse. Then as I began to climb the ladder within my family's company, I started to notice some similarities between corporate tactics and martial arts. This is where I began to research what corporate manoeuvres our competitors were using and how I could translate them into martial arts moves so that I could reverse engineer how the "fight" could end up and try to guide it in the direction that I wanted.

These findings were then implemented in my own businesses as well as the family company so that we could assess how the competitors reacted and how best to implement the strategy.

This was the beginning of the corporate sabaki concept.

1.

Introduction: The Intersection of Martial Arts and Business Strategy

In the ever-evolving landscape of business where agility, anticipation, and adaptability are crucial for success, drawing inspiration from unexpected sources can provide fresh perspectives. One key method is the sabaki method, a fundamental concept in Ashihara Karate, which emphasizes movement and positioning to turn an opponent's strength into a weakness. This book explores how the principles of sabaki can be adapted to business strategy, offering unique insights into navigating competitive environments, making strategic decisions, and achieving sustainable success.

Understanding Sabaki: The Core Concepts

Sabaki, a Japanese term meaning "to handle" or "to manage," is a pivotal concept in Ashihara Karate, a style known for its practical approach to self-defense. Unlike traditional Karate, which often relies on direct confrontation, Ashihara Karate focuses on using an opponent's energy and momentum to one's advantage. This is achieved through a combination of evasion, redirection, and counterattack, all while maintaining balance and control.

The key principles of sabaki include:

1. Movement and Positioning: Rather than meeting an attack head-on, practitioners of sabaki seek to move to a more advantageous position, often to the side or behind the opponent. This not only avoids the force of the attack but also opens up opportunities for counterattack.

2. Timing and Anticipation: Successful application of sabaki requires precise timing and anticipation of the opponent's moves. This involves reading subtle cues and reacting quickly to changes in the situation.

3. Flexibility and Adaptability: Sabaki encourages flexibility in both thought and action. Practitioners must be able to adapt their strategies on the fly, responding to unexpected developments with agility and creativity.

4. Economy of Motion: Efficiency is a key focus of sabaki. Every movement is purposeful, with no wasted energy. This principle underscores the importance of being economical in action, using only what is necessary to achieve the desired outcome.

Translating Sabaki into Business Strategy

The principles of sabaki are applicable in the boardroom. In the complex world of business, companies often face challenges that require them to be agile, anticipate changes, and adapt quickly to new circumstances. The following sections explore how each of the core concepts of sabaki can be applied to business strategy.

Movement and Positioning in Business

In martial arts, proper positioning can turn the tide of a confrontation. Similarly, in business, strategic positioning is crucial for gaining a competitive advantage. Companies must identify and occupy market positions that play to their strengths whilst exploiting competitors' weaknesses. This involves:

1. Market Segmentation: Identifying and targeting specific market segments where the company's products or services can thrive. By understanding customer needs and preferences, businesses can position themselves in niches that are underserved or overlooked by competitors.

2. Differentiation: Creating a unique value proposition that sets the company apart from the competition. This could be through innovative products, exceptional customer service, or a strong brand identity.

3. Strategic Partnerships: Forming alliances and partnerships can help a company access new markets, share resources, and leverage complementary strengths. Just as in sabaki, where practitioners seek to move into advantageous

positions, businesses must align themselves with partners that enhance their strategic positioning.

Timing and Anticipation in Business

In Ashihara Karate, anticipating an opponent's moves is key to executing successful counterattacks. In business, companies that can anticipate market trends and shifts in consumer behaviour are better positioned to capitalize on emerging opportunities and mitigate risks.

1. Market Research and Analysis: Conducting thorough market research and analysis is essential for understanding industry trends, customer preferences, and competitor strategies. This information allows businesses to anticipate changes and adapt their strategies accordingly.

2. Scenario Planning: By envisioning various future scenarios and preparing for them, companies can develop contingency plans and be ready to respond to unexpected events. This proactive approach helps businesses stay ahead of the curve and avoid being caught off guard by market disruptions.

3. Agile Decision-Making: In a rapidly changing business environment, the ability to make quick, informed decisions is crucial. A martial artist must react swiftly to an opponent's movements, business leaders must also be able to pivot and make strategic decisions on the fly.

Flexibility and Adaptability in Business

The principle of flexibility and adaptability is central to both sabaki and business strategy. In martial arts, rigid adherence to a single approach can lead to defeat. Similarly, businesses must be willing to adapt their strategies in response to changing circumstances.

1. Continuous Improvement: Adopting a mindset of continuous improvement allows businesses to learn from their experiences and make incremental adjustments to their strategies. This involves regularly reviewing performance, seeking feedback, and being open to change.

2. Innovation and Experimentation: Encouraging innovation and experimentation is key to staying competitive. Companies that foster a culture of creativity and are willing to take calculated risks are better equipped to adapt to new market conditions and seize opportunities.

3. Resilience and Agility: Building a resilient organization that can withstand shocks and adapt to change is critical for long-term success. This involves developing a flexible workforce, investing in technology, and fostering a culture of agility and responsiveness.

Economy of Motion in Business

Efficiency is a cornerstone of sabaki, and it is equally important in business. In a competitive market, companies must use their resources wisely and avoid unnecessary expenditures.

1. Lean Operations: Implementing lean principles can help businesses streamline their operations, reduce waste, and improve efficiency. This involves optimizing processes, eliminating procedural

redundancies, and focusing on activities that add value.

2. Resource Allocation: Effective resource allocation is essential for maximizing returns on investment. Companies must prioritize their resources, including time, money, and personnel, and allocate them to areas with the highest potential for growth and profitability.

3. Cost Management: Keeping costs under control is crucial for maintaining profitability. Businesses should regularly review their cost structures, identify areas where expenses can be reduced, and implement cost-saving measures without compromising quality.

The Importance of Agility, Anticipation, and Adaptability in Business

The principles of sabaki highlight the importance of agility, anticipation, and adaptability in both martial arts and business. In a world where change is constant and competition is fierce, these qualities are essential for survival and success.

- Agility: A martial artist must be agile to avoid and counter attacks, similarly businesses must be nimble and responsive to changing market conditions. This requires a flexible organizational structure, a willingness to innovate, and the ability to pivot quickly when necessary.

- Anticipation: The ability to anticipate and prepare for future challenges and opportunities is a key advantage in both martial arts and business. Companies that can foresee market trends and consumer behaviour are better positioned to stay ahead of the competition and capitalize on new opportunities.

- <u>Adaptability:</u> In both martial arts and business, the ability to adapt to new situations is critical. This involves being open to change, learning from experiences, and continuously evolving strategies to stay relevant and competitive.

The Sabaki Method as a Blueprint for Business Strategy

The sabaki method in Ashihara Karate offers a rich source of inspiration for business strategy. By embracing the principles of movement and positioning, timing and anticipation, flexibility and adaptability, and economy of motion, businesses can navigate complex environments, outmanoeuvre competitors, and achieve long-term success.

As with martial arts, mastering these principles requires practice, discipline, and a commitment to continuous improvement. Companies that cultivate a culture of agility, anticipation, and adaptability will be well-equipped to face the challenges of the modern business world and emerge as leaders in their industries.

The sabaki method provides a powerful framework for understanding and navigating the dynamics of competition and change. By applying these martial arts principles to business strategy, companies can develop the agility, foresight, and resilience needed to thrive in an ever-changing landscape. Just as a skilled martial artist uses sabaki to turn an opponent's strength into a weakness, businesses can use these principles to turn challenges into opportunities and achieve sustainable success.

2.

Understanding Sabaki: The Core Principles

Sabaki, a term often associated with the martial arts world, particularly Ashihara Karate, represents a sophisticated and strategic approach to combat. Originating from the Japanese word meaning "handling" or "management," sabaki involves the skilful manipulation of an opponent's force and movement to gain a strategic advantage. It is not merely a physical technique but a mindset that emphasizes adaptability, efficiency, and precision.

In Karate, sabaki is a core principle that distinguishes modern styles from others. It focuses on evading or redirecting an opponent's attack rather than meeting force with force. This approach not only conserves energy but also allows practitioners to control and dominate the fight. Beyond martial arts, the principles of sabaki have profound implications for various fields, including business, where strategic thinking and adaptability are crucial.

The Fundamental Principles of Sabaki
Redirecting Force
One of the foundational principles of sabaki is the concept of redirecting force. In a martial arts context, this means using an opponent's momentum against them, rather than directly opposing it. This principle is not only efficient but also effective, as it requires less energy and can quickly unbalance an opponent.

In Ashihara Karate, practitioners are trained to anticipate and read an opponent's movements. By positioning themselves at an angle and using circular motions, they can deflect attacks and create openings for counter-attacks. For example, instead of blocking a punch directly, a practitioner might step off the line of attack and use a circular motion to guide the opponent's arm away, leaving them exposed to a counter-strike.

This principle is vividly illustrated in the example of an experienced karate practitioner who faces a much larger and stronger opponent. Instead of trying to outmuscle the opponent, they use sabaki to deflect the incoming attacks, using the opponent's force against them. By redirecting the opponent's punches and kicks, they conserve energy and wait for the right moment to counter-attack, eventually leading to victory.

Positioning
Positioning is another critical aspect of sabaki. It involves placing oneself in the most advantageous spot relative to the opponent, often at an angle that makes it difficult for the opponent to launch an effective attack. Good positioning not only helps in defence but also sets up opportunities for offensive manoeuvres.

In Ashihara Karate, the emphasis is on finding the "blind spot" of the opponent, a position where the opponent cannot easily see or attack. This concept is crucial in both sparring and real-life self-defence situations. By moving to the opponent's side or back, a practitioner can evade attacks and launch counters from a position of safety and control.

An anecdote from a karate tournament highlights the importance of positioning. A competitor, known for his agility, consistently outmanoeuvred his opponents by staying just out of reach and striking from unexpected angles. His mastery of positioning made him a formidable opponent, as he could control the pace and flow of the match, dictating when and where the exchanges occurred.

Timing
Timing is the third fundamental principle of sabaki. It involves knowing when to act, whether to evade, block, or counter-attack. Proper timing can turn the tide of a confrontation, allowing a practitioner to capitalize on the opponent's mistakes or momentary lapses in defence.

In Ashihara Karate, practitioners learn to read the rhythm of a fight, waiting for the perfect moment to strike. This can involve delaying a counter-attack to catch the opponent off guard or executing a move just as the opponent commits to an attack, leaving them vulnerable.

An example from a street self-defence scenario illustrates the importance of timing. A practitioner, confronted by an aggressive individual, remains calm and waits for the attacker to make the first move. As the attacker lunges, the practitioner sidesteps and uses the attacker's momentum to throw them to the ground, ending the confrontation swiftly. This precise timing not only avoided unnecessary violence but also ensured the practitioner's safety.

Application of Sabaki Principles in Business

The principles of sabaki can be applied effectively in the business world. Similarly to martial arts, business strategies often involve navigating challenges, managing conflicts, and seizing opportunities. The concepts of redirecting force, positioning, and timing can provide valuable insights for business leaders and strategists.

Redirecting Force in Business
In a business context, redirecting force can be seen as turning challenges into opportunities. For instance, a company facing a sudden market shift can use it as a chance to innovate and pivot its offerings. By understanding the market's momentum and adapting accordingly, businesses can gain a competitive edge.

One example could be a tech company that faced declining demand for its core product. Instead of resisting the market trend, the company redirected its efforts towards emerging technologies, leveraging its existing expertise to enter a new market segment. This strategic pivot allowed the company to not only survive but thrive in a changing landscape.

Positioning in Business
Positioning in business is about finding the right niche and differentiating oneself from competitors. As in martial arts, where good positioning can neutralize an opponent's strengths, in business a strong market position can make a company less vulnerable to competitive pressures.

Consider the idea of a startup entering a crowded market. By identifying an underserved niche and positioning its products uniquely, the startup can carve out a loyal customer base. For example, a new entrant in the fitness industry might focus on providing eco-friendly workout gear, appealing to environmentally conscious consumers. This strategic positioning allows the company to stand out and attract a specific demographic, therefore reducing direct competition.

Timing in Business

Timing is crucial in business decisions, whether launching a new product, entering a market, or responding to a competitor's move. Just as in martial arts, where striking at the right moment can be decisive, in business, timely actions can lead to success.

A well-known strategy is the launch of a new tech gadget that coincides perfectly with a holiday season, thus allowing the company to capture significant market share. The company's timing capitalizes on increased consumer spending during the holidays, maximizing sales and brand visibility. Conversely, poor timing can lead to missed opportunities or, worse, significant losses.

The principles of sabaki—redirecting force, positioning, and timing—are not only fundamental to martial arts but also offer valuable lessons for various aspects of life. By understanding and applying these principles, individuals can navigate challenges more effectively, make strategic decisions, and achieve their goals.

In both martial arts and business, the essence of sabaki lies in adaptability, awareness, and precision. It teaches us to move with the flow of events, rather than against them, and to find the most efficient and effective path to success. Whether in a dojo or a boardroom, the wisdom of sabaki can guide us towards a more strategic and mindful approach to challenges and opportunities.

3.

From Dojo to Boardroom: Translating Martial Arts into Business Tactics

When comparing martial arts and business, the dojo and the boardroom often serve as arenas for honing similar skills. The discipline, focus, and strategic thinking cultivated in martial arts training offer valuable insights and tools for navigating the challenges of the business world. This chapter explores the parallels between these two domains and examines how principles from the dojo can translate into effective business tactics. We will also highlight successful business leaders who have drawn from their martial arts experiences to excel in their careers.

The Discipline of Training: Building a Strong Foundation

Consistency and Routine
In martial arts, consistent practice is essential for mastery. This dedication to routine fosters discipline and perseverance, and is equally important in business. Similarly, a martial artist trains regularly to perfect techniques, business professionals must continuously refine their skills and adapt to changing environments.

Goal Setting and Achievement
Martial artists often set short-term and long-term goals, such as achieving a certain belt level or mastering a specific technique. This goal-oriented mindset is crucial in business, where setting clear objectives and devising strategies to achieve them are foundational to success.

Embracing the Basics
In the dojo, mastery of fundamental techniques is crucial. Similarly, in business, understanding and mastering the basics—such as financial literacy, communication, and leadership—provide a strong foundation for more complex tasks.

Focus and Mindfulness: The Power of Being Present

Mind-Body Connection
Martial arts training emphasizes the connection between the mind and body, promoting awareness and mindfulness. This heightened awareness is valuable in business, where staying present and focused can lead to better decision-making and crisis management.

Handling Pressure
Sparring in martial arts teaches practitioners to stay calm and composed under pressure. This ability to maintain focus and clarity is directly applicable to high-stakes business situations, where leaders must make critical decisions swiftly and effectively.

Visualization and Mental Rehearsal
Martial artists often use visualization techniques to mentally rehearse their moves. This practice can be applied in business settings, where visualizing success and preparing for potential challenges can enhance performance and outcomes.

Strategic Thinking: Anticipation and Adaptation

Reading the Opponent
In martial arts, understanding the opponent's moves and intentions is crucial. This skill of reading and anticipating can be translated into business strategy, where analysing competitors and market trends helps businesses stay ahead.

1. Adaptability and Flexibility
   Martial arts teach adaptability, as practitioners must adjust their techniques based on the opponent's actions. Similarly, in business, being flexible and willing to pivot strategies in response to market changes is key to long-term success.

2. Risk Assessment and Decision Making
   Both martial arts and business require assessing risks and making decisions quickly. The ability to weigh

options, consider potential outcomes, and take calculated risks is a valuable skill that can lead to significant business achievements.

Real-World Applications: Lessons from Business Leaders

Tony Robbins: Strategic Intervention
Tony Robbins, a renowned life coach and entrepreneur, holds a black belt in Jhoon Rhee Taekwondo [1]. It is safe to assume that his martial arts training is a positive influence on strategic intervention and personal development. Robbins often speaks about the importance of mental and physical conditioning, emphasizing the role of discipline and resilience in achieving success.

Hideyuki Ashihara: Focus and Tenacity
Hideyuki Ashihara, the founder of Ashihara Karate, held a 9th degree black belt in Kyokushin. During his time as one of the key members of that style whilst helping to grow the karate style into many different cities in Japan, he was involved in a street fight where he was attacked by 5 thugs. He defeated them all but got in trouble by the Kyokushin Honbu for attracting police attention and was temporarily suspended from the club [2]. During the suspension he began to refine the Sabaki method and when the suspension was lifted, he began to become renowned for his new methodology. He eventually started his own style to focus on these new methods in 1980 and managed to grow his new karate style from 1 dojo in Matsuyama to now a significant 220 Ashihara dojos around the world [3]. A lot of these dojos were started with the help of his son Hidenori Ashihara after Hideyuki passed away.

Takeda Shingen: Adaptability and Resilience

Takeda Shingen, a Japanese samurai and Daimyo (feudal lord) had extensive martial arts abilities. He was known as a famous samurai and strong warrior. He was born into the powerful Takeda family who were shugo daimyo (military governors) that controlled the Kai province (present day yamanashi prefecture) of Japan. This province had little arable land and was located in a mountainous territory so it wasn't the most valuable or well-regarded territory. With goals of expansion through his leadership he was able to assume control of Shinano province (present day Nagano prefecture), and other adjacent land to Kai province along with making large in roads into land controlled by Tokugawa Ieyasu which is in present day Shizuoka prefecture. Takeda Shingen was known as one of the most powerful Daimyo at the time in Japan and was a master at using government legislation and control tactics to expand his territory. [4]

The lessons learned in the dojo extend far beyond the practice of martial arts. The discipline, focus, and strategic thinking developed through martial arts training are invaluable assets in the business world. By embracing these principles, business professionals can cultivate a mindset that fosters growth, innovation, and resilience. As illustrated by the experiences of successful business leaders, the connection between martial arts and business is not merely theoretical but a practical guide to achieving excellence in both arenas. There is a good quote by Hideyuki Ashihara: "Everything in life can be worked on in the dojo, a strong mind, strong body and a vital spirit".

4.

The Philosophy of Movement: Navigating Business Challenges

In martial arts, the concept of movement transcends mere physical actions; it embodies a philosophy of adaptation, resilience, and strategic thinking. Similarly, in the business world, companies must navigate an ever-changing landscape with agility and foresight. The parallels between martial arts movements and business strategy can be seen in the emphasizing of the importance of fluidity, adaptability, and flexibility in responding to market changes. Through this lens, we will examine how businesses can learn from martial arts to thrive in a dynamic environment.

The Essence of Movement in Martial Arts

Movement in martial arts is a multifaceted concept encompassing physical, mental, and strategic dimensions. It is not merely about executing techniques but also about anticipating and reacting to an opponent's actions. Martial artists are trained to read subtle cues, adjust their stances, and employ techniques that capitalize on the opponent's weaknesses. This requires a high degree of awareness, precision, and fluidity.

Fluidity in martial arts is the ability to move seamlessly and adapt to changing situations. It involves not just physical agility but also mental flexibility. Martial artists must be prepared to switch strategies in an instant, responding to the dynamic flow of combat. This principle of fluidity is equally applicable in business, where companies must navigate complex and unpredictable markets.

Fluidity in Business

Fluidity in business refers to the capacity to remain open to change and not be rigidly attached to a single path or strategy. In today's fast-paced world, markets evolve rapidly, and customer preferences can shift overnight. Companies that are rigid in their approach often struggle to keep up, while those that embrace fluidity can adapt and thrive.

A prime example of business fluidity is Netflix. Originally a DVD rental service, Netflix foresaw the decline of physical media and the rise of digital streaming. Instead of clinging to its original business model, Netflix made a bold pivot to become a streaming service. This move required significant investment in technology and content but ultimately positioned Netflix as a leader in the entertainment industry. The company's willingness to embrace change and innovate continuously has allowed it to remain at the forefront of a highly competitive market.

Fluidity also involves being open to new ideas and experimenting with different approaches. Companies that foster a culture of innovation encourage employees to think creatively and explore new possibilities. This culture of experimentation can lead to breakthrough products and services that differentiate a company from its competitors.

Adaptability: The Key to Survival

In martial arts, adaptability is crucial for survival. Martial artists must be able to adjust their techniques and strategies based on the opponent's actions. This requires a keen understanding of one's strengths and weaknesses, as well as the ability to quickly analyse the opponent's movements and intentions.

Similarly, in business, adaptability is a key determinant of success. Companies that can quickly adapt to changing market conditions, customer preferences, and technological advancements are more likely to thrive. Conversely, those that fail to adapt often struggle or even fail.

The contrasting stories of Kodak and Fujifilm illustrate the importance of adaptability. Kodak, once a dominant player in the photography industry, failed to adapt to the digital revolution. Despite being a pioneer in digital photography, Kodak was slow to transition from film to digital, fearing it would cannibalize its profitable film business. As a result, the company lost its market leadership and eventually filed for bankruptcy.

In contrast, Fujifilm successfully navigated the shift to digital photography by diversifying its business. Recognizing the decline of film, Fujifilm invested in new technologies and expanded into healthcare, cosmetics, and other fields. This adaptability allowed Fujifilm to not only survive but also thrive in a rapidly changing industry.

Adaptability also involves being responsive to customer needs. Companies that actively listen to their customers and adjust their products and services accordingly are more likely to succeed. This customer-centric approach helps businesses build loyalty and trust, which are critical for long-term success.

Flexibility: Embracing the Unexpected

Flexibility in martial arts is the ability to respond effectively to unexpected situations. Martial artists train to be flexible in their techniques, allowing them to counter opponents' moves and adapt to various scenarios. This flexibility is not just physical but also mental, as martial artists must remain calm and composed in the face of uncertainty.

In the business world, flexibility is equally important. Companies must be prepared to handle unexpected challenges, such as economic downturns, supply chain disruptions, or sudden shifts in consumer behaviour. Those that are flexible in their operations and strategies are better equipped to navigate these challenges.

Apple Inc. is a prime example of a company that has demonstrated flexibility. Over the years, Apple has expanded its product lines beyond computers to include smartphones, tablets, wearables, and services. This flexibility has allowed Apple to tap into new markets and revenue streams, making it one of the most valuable companies in the world.

Flexibility also involves being open to new business models and partnerships. For example, when the COVID-19 pandemic disrupted traditional retail, many companies quickly adapted by enhancing their online presence and exploring new sales channels. This flexibility enabled businesses to continue serving customers and generating revenue despite the challenges posed by the pandemic.

Movement and Strategy: The Sabaki Method

The sabaki method in martial arts focuses on movement and positioning to gain an advantage over the opponent. It involves redirecting the opponent's force and using it to one's benefit. This strategic approach allows martial artists to conserve energy and maintain control of the fight.

In business, the concept of sabaki can be applied to strategic positioning. Companies that position themselves effectively in the market can leverage their strengths and capitalize on opportunities. This involves understanding market trends, identifying competitive advantages, and anticipating potential challenges.

Tesla's entry into the electric vehicle (EV) market is an example of strategic positioning. Tesla identified a growing demand for environmentally friendly transportation and positioned itself as a leader in the EV market. The company invested heavily in technology and infrastructure, such as charging stations, to support its vision. Tesla's strategic positioning has not only disrupted the automotive industry but also set the standard for innovation in electric vehicles.

Strategic positioning also involves understanding the competitive landscape. Companies that can anticipate competitors' moves and adjust their strategies accordingly are more likely to succeed. This requires a deep understanding of the market and the ability to think several steps ahead.

The Balance of Offensive and Defensive Strategies

In martial arts, a balanced approach that includes both offensive and defensive techniques is crucial for success. Martial artists must know when to attack and when to defend, adjusting their strategies based on the situation. This balance ensures they can effectively respond to threats while also seizing opportunities.

Similarly, businesses must balance offensive and defensive strategies. Offensive strategies, such as innovation and market expansion, allow companies to grow and gain a competitive edge. Defensive strategies, such as risk management and cost control, help protect the company from potential threats and downturns.

Amazon exemplifies a company that effectively balances offensive and defensive strategies. On the offensive side, Amazon continuously innovates by expanding its product offerings and entering new markets, such as cloud computing with Amazon Web Services (AWS). On the defensive side, Amazon invests in logistics and supply chain management to ensure efficient and reliable delivery to customers. This balanced approach has enabled Amazon to become a dominant player in e-commerce and beyond.

Balancing offensive and defensive strategies also involve making tough decisions about resource allocation. Companies must prioritize investments that drive growth while also ensuring they have sufficient resources to weather downturns or unexpected challenges. This requires careful planning and a deep understanding of the company's strengths and weaknesses.

Lessons from Successful Businesses

The success stories of companies like Netflix, Fujifilm, Apple, Tesla, and Amazon offer valuable lessons for businesses seeking to navigate a dynamic environment. These companies have demonstrated fluidity, adaptability, flexibility, and strategic positioning, enabling them to thrive in the face of change.

One key lesson is the importance of continuous learning and innovation. Successful companies are always looking for ways to improve and stay ahead of the competition. This involves investing in research and development, exploring new markets, and staying attuned to customer needs.

Another lesson is the value of a customer-centric approach. Companies that prioritize customer satisfaction and build strong relationships with their customers are more likely to achieve long-term success. This involves actively listening to feedback, providing exceptional service, and continually enhancing the customer experience.

Finally, successful companies understand the importance of strategic agility. They are not afraid to pivot or make bold moves when necessary. This requires a willingness to take calculated risks and the ability to execute strategies effectively.

The principles of movement in martial arts—fluidity, adaptability, flexibility, and strategic positioning—offer valuable insights for navigating business challenges. Just as martial artists must be agile and responsive, businesses must be prepared to adapt to a constantly changing environment. By embracing these principles, companies can position themselves for success, even in the face of uncertainty.

In a world where change is the only constant, businesses that embody the spirit of martial arts movement will not only survive but also thrive. Whether it's anticipating market trends, responding to customer needs, or seizing new opportunities, the ability to move with grace and agility is the key to staying ahead in the competitive landscape.

It is clear that the art of movement in martial arts is more than just physical—it is a mindset and a strategy. In the same way, businesses must cultivate a mindset of continuous improvement and a strategy of dynamic adaptation. By doing so, they can navigate the complexities of the modern market and achieve lasting success.

5.

Reading the Opponent: Market Analysis and Competitor Insight

Understanding the competition is crucial for success. A martial artist studies their opponent to anticipate moves and counter them, similarly businesses must closely observe their competitors to stay ahead in the market. This analogy underscores the importance of strategic insight and adaptability, key components in navigating the complexities of the business world.

The techniques and strategies for market analysis and competitive intelligence can draw parallels with martial arts principles and what you can do to implement these in your life or business.

The Art of Reading the Opponent: A Martial Arts Perspective

In martial arts, reading an opponent is a skill that involves observing their movements, anticipating their actions, and understanding their strengths and weaknesses. Techniques such as *feints*, *timing*, and *positioning* are employed to gain an advantage. Similarly, in business, companies must observe their competitors, understand market trends, and anticipate changes to maintain a competitive edge.

Just as a martial artist might use sparring to test and refine their skills, businesses can engage in competitive analysis to better understand the market landscape. This involves not only identifying competitors but also analysing their strategies, strengths, and weaknesses. By doing so, companies can position themselves effectively, making strategic moves that capitalize on market opportunities and mitigate threats.

Techniques for Market Analysis and Competitive Intelligence

1. Market Research: Market research involves gathering and analysing data about the market, including customer preferences, market size, and trends. This information helps businesses understand the landscape in which they operate and identify potential opportunities and threats.

2. SWOT Analysis: A SWOT analysis is a strategic planning tool used to identify a company's Strengths, Weaknesses, Opportunities, and Threats. By evaluating these factors, businesses can develop strategies that leverage their strengths, address their weaknesses, capitalize on opportunities, and mitigate threats.

3. <u>Porter's Five Forces:</u> Porter's Five Forces framework helps businesses analyse the competitive forces in an industry: the intensity of competitive rivalry, the threat of new entrants, the threat of substitutes, the bargaining power of buyers, and the bargaining power of suppliers. This analysis helps companies understand the dynamics of their industry and develop strategies to improve their competitive position.

4. <u>Competitor Profiling:</u> Competitor profiling involves identifying key competitors and analysing their strategies, strengths, and weaknesses. This analysis can include examining competitors' products, pricing, marketing strategies, and customer service. By understanding their competitors, businesses can differentiate themselves and develop strategies to outperform them.

5. <u>Benchmarking:</u> Benchmarking involves comparing a company's practices and performance metrics with those of leading companies in the industry. This process helps businesses identify areas for improvement and adopt best practices to enhance their performance.

6. <u>Data Analytics and Big Data:</u> Data analytics and big data enable businesses to gain insights into market trends, customer behaviour, and competitor strategies. By analysing large volumes of data, companies can identify patterns and trends that inform strategic decision-making.

7. <u>Customer Feedback and Social Listening:</u> Gathering customer feedback and engaging in social listening allows businesses to understand customer needs and

preferences. This information can be used to improve products and services, as well as to monitor competitors' activities and reputation.

Case Studies

Apple vs. Samsung: Apple and Samsung are two of the biggest players in the smartphone market. Apple has consistently differentiated itself through innovation and design, while Samsung has focused on offering a wide range of products to cater to different customer segments. By understanding their competition and the market, both companies have been able to maintain a strong presence in the industry.

Netflix vs. Blockbuster: Netflix's rise and Blockbuster's fall is a classic example of how understanding market trends and competitor weaknesses can lead to success. Netflix recognized the shift towards digital streaming and subscription-based models, while Blockbuster failed to adapt. Netflix's keen observation and strategic insight allowed it to disrupt the market and become a dominant player.

Toyota vs. General Motors: Toyota's implementation of lean manufacturing and continuous improvement (kaizen) allowed it to outperform General Motors in terms of efficiency and quality. By focusing on eliminating waste and improving processes, Toyota gained a competitive edge, eventually becoming the world's largest automaker.

Walmart vs. Kmart USA: Walmart's focus on supply chain efficiency and cost leadership enabled it to outmanoeuvre Kmart, which struggled with higher costs and less efficient operations. Walmart's understanding of the importance of cost control and its ability to leverage its supply chain allowed it to dominate the American retail market.

Strategic Insight and Decision Making

The ability to observe and analyse competitors is a critical skill in business. It allows companies to anticipate market shifts, identify opportunities, and avoid potential pitfalls. Developing strategic insight involves not only having an understanding of the current competitive landscape but also anticipating future changes. Companies must be proactive, continuously monitoring the market and adapting their strategies as needed.

Using insights from market analysis and competitive research into decision-making processes can lead to more informed and effective strategies. This proactive approach ensures that businesses are well-prepared to navigate challenges and seize opportunities, ultimately leading to sustained success.

Understanding the competition in business is akin to reading an opponent in martial arts. It requires keen observation, strategic insight, and the ability to adapt to changing circumstances. By employing techniques such as market research, SWOT analysis, and competitor profiling, businesses can gain a comprehensive understanding of the market and their competitors.

The case studies of companies like Apple, Netflix, Toyota, and Walmart demonstrate the power of strategic insight and the importance of staying ahead of the competition. By learning from these examples and continuously honing their competitive intelligence, businesses can position themselves for long-term success in an ever-evolving market landscape.

Mastering the art of understanding competition is essential for any business seeking to thrive in business. Just as a skilled martial artist must read their opponent, businesses must remain vigilant, agile, and strategic in their approach to competition. This combination of observation, analysis, and proactive decision-making is the key to outmanoeuvring competitors and achieving success.

6.

**Strategic Positioning:
Finding the Right Stance in
Business**

In both martial arts and business, success hinges on strategic positioning. A martial artist must adopt the right stance to defend, attack, and adapt to their opponent's moves; the same as a business must find its optimal market position to thrive in a competitive landscape. Let's jump into how businesses can identify their strengths and leverage them for a competitive advantage, drawing parallels with martial arts stances and strategies.

The Importance of Stance in Martial Arts

In martial arts, the stance is more than just a physical posture; it embodies a fundamental strategic position that can influence the outcome of a fight. Each stance—whether it's the aggressive front stance, the balanced horse stance, or the defensive back stance—serves a specific purpose and offers unique advantages. For instance:

1. Front Stance (Zenkutsu-dachi): Provides stability and power for forward attacks and can quickly transition into offensive or defensive moves.

2. Horse Stance (Kibadachi): Offers strength and stability, ideal for both blocking and striking.

3. Back Stance (Kokutsu-dachi): Emphasizes defence and is perfect for countering attacks while maintaining a strong base.

Choosing the right stance in martial arts is crucial for optimizing performance, just as choosing the right market position is essential for a business's success.

Identifying Your Business's Strengths

To position a business effectively, it is essential to first identify its strengths. Much like a martial artist evaluates their physical and technical advantages; businesses must assess their unique attributes. Here's how businesses can identify their strengths:

1. Conduct a SWOT Analysis: A SWOT (Strengths, Weaknesses, Opportunities, Threats) analysis helps businesses pinpoint internal strengths and weaknesses. For instance, a company may have a strong brand reputation, innovative technology, or a dedicated customer base.

2. <u>Analyse Competencies:</u> Determine what your company does best. This could be exceptional customer service, unique product features, or operational efficiency.

3. <u>Gather Feedback:</u> Customer and employee feedback can provide insights into what the business excels at and where it can improve.

Apple Inc. excels in product design, user experience, and brand loyalty. By leveraging these strengths, Apple has established a dominant position in the technology market. Its focus on high-quality, aesthetically pleasing products and a seamless business ecosystem differentiates it from competitors.

Leveraging Strengths for Market Positioning

Once strengths are identified, the next step is to leverage them to create a compelling market position. This is akin to a martial artist choosing a stance that best utilizes their skills and advantages.

1. <u>Develop a Unique Value Proposition (UVP):</u> Your UVP should clearly communicate how your business's strengths meet the needs of your target market better than competitors. This proposition is your equivalent of choosing the optimal stance for a fight.

2. <u>Focus on Niche Markets:</u> Sometimes, the best stance is a specialized one. Targeting niche markets where your strengths are particularly relevant can provide a competitive edge.

3. <u>Continuously Adapt:</u> A martial artist adapts their stance based on the opponent's movements, it is vital that businesses must also remain flexible and adjust their positioning as market conditions change.

Tesla has leveraged its strengths in electric vehicle technology and sustainable energy solutions to carve out a unique position in the automotive industry. By focusing on innovation and environmental impact, Tesla has differentiated itself from traditional car manufacturers.

Analysing the Competition

Understanding the competition is crucial for effective market positioning. This involves studying competitors' strengths, weaknesses, and positioning strategies. In martial arts, this is similar to analysing an opponent's stance and tactics to anticipate their moves.

1. Competitive Analysis: Research competitors to understand their market position, strengths, and weaknesses. Tools like market research reports, customer reviews, and competitor websites can provide valuable insights.

2. Benchmarking: Compare your business's performance with industry standards and best practices. This can help identify areas where you can gain a competitive advantage.

Nike and Adidas both dominate the sportswear market but employ different strategies. Nike focuses on innovation and endorsement deals, while Adidas emphasizes sustainability and collaborations with designers. By understanding these strategies, each company positions itself to leverage its unique strengths.

Case Studies of Successful Market Positioning

Let's explore some successful market positioning strategies and how they relate to finding the right stance:

Amazon:
Amazon initially positioned itself as an online bookstore but

leveraged its strengths in logistics and technology to expand into a global e-commerce powerhouse. Its emphasis on convenience, fast delivery, and a vast product range has set it apart from competitors.

Red Bull:
Red Bull's market positioning is built around its association with extreme sports and high-energy lifestyles. By focusing on this niche and sponsoring related events, Red Bull has created a strong brand identity and loyal customer base.

Starbucks:
Starbucks positioned itself as a premium coffee experience rather than just a coffee shop. Its ability to create a unique store ambiance and offering a range of high-quality beverages have set it apart from other coffee retailers.

The Role of Adaptability in Market Positioning

In both martial arts and business, the ability to adapt is crucial. Just as a martial artist must adjust their stance based on the opponent's movements, businesses must be agile in response to market changes.

1. <u>Monitor Market Trends:</u> Keep an eye on industry trends and consumer preferences. Adapting to these trends can help maintain a competitive edge.

2. <u>Be Ready to Pivot:</u> If a particular market position isn't yielding the desired results, be prepared to pivot and explore new opportunities.

Netflix's initial market position was as a DVD rental service. However, as technology and consumer preferences shifted, Netflix pivoted to streaming and original content production, allowing it to become a leader in the entertainment industry.

Finding the right stance in martial arts and positioning a business in the market both require careful strategic planning, and adaptability. By identifying strengths and leveraging them effectively while staying current with competitors and market trends, businesses can achieve a competitive advantage similar to a martial artist's optimal stance.

As both martial artists and business leaders navigate their respective arenas, the principles of strategic positioning and adaptability remain central to their success. Embracing these principles can lead to remarkable achievements, whether in the dojo or the boardroom.

7.

Timing and Distance: The Art of Strategic Decision Making

Timing and distance are two fundamental concepts in martial arts that determine the outcome of any engagement. These principles are equally critical in the business world, where understanding the right moment to act and maintaining a strategic distance from competitors can spell the difference between success and failure. This section delves into how businesses can optimize their decision-making processes by applying the lessons of timing and distance from martial arts, complete with real-world examples to illustrate these points.

The Essence of Timing and Distance in Martial Arts

In martial arts, timing refers to the ability to execute techniques at the most opportune moment, maximizing their effectiveness. Distance, or maai in Japanese martial arts, is the spatial relationship between opponents. Proper management of distance allows a martial artist to control the engagement, dictating the flow of the encounter and minimizing vulnerability.

Both timing and distance are interdependent; a well-timed strike is ineffective if the distance is misjudged, and maintaining the right distance is futile without the ability to exploit the right moment. Mastery of these concepts enables martial artists to anticipate and counter their opponent's moves, turning the tide of combat in their favour.

Translating Martial Arts Principles to Business Strategy

In business, timing and distance manifest in various forms, from market entry and product launches to competitive positioning and strategic partnerships. Companies that excel in these areas can anticipate market trends, outmanoeuvre competitors, and seize opportunities with precision.

Timing: The Art of Strategic Decision-Making

1. Market Entry and Product Launches:
   Entering a market or launching a product at the right time can make or break a business. For instance, Apple's timing with the iPhone launch in 2007 was impeccable. The company capitalized on advancements in technology and a growing demand for smartphones, disrupting the market and establishing a dominant position.

Similarly, Netflix's transition from DVD rentals to streaming in the late 2000s came at a time when internet speeds and consumer preferences were aligning with streaming services. By recognizing and acting on this opportune moment, Netflix transformed itself into a global entertainment powerhouse.

2. <u>Responding to Market Trends:</u>
Businesses must be adept at reading market signals and adjusting their strategies accordingly. Zara, the Spanish fast-fashion retailer, exemplifies this with its agile supply chain that allows it to respond to fashion trends rapidly. By optimizing the timing of its product releases, Zara can keep its inventory fresh and aligned with current consumer preferences, maintaining a competitive edge in the fast-paced fashion industry. This isn't always the most sustainable strategy but it does demonstrate this point very well.

3. <u>Crisis Management:</u>
Effective crisis management hinges on timely decision-making. During the 2018 data breach scandal, Facebook's delayed response exacerbated the situation, leading to significant reputational damage [5]. In contrast, Johnson & Johnson's swift and transparent handling of the 1982 Tylenol crisis is often cited as a textbook example of timely crisis management. By quickly recalling the product and communicating openly with the public, the company managed to restore consumer trust and safeguard its

brand [6].

Distance: Maintaining Strategic Positioning

1. Competitive Positioning:
   Equally as a martial artist controls distance to manage engagements, businesses must maintain a strategic distance from competitors to protect their market position. This involves identifying and occupying a market niche that differentiates them from rivals. Muttley's Estate, for example, has carved out a distinct position in the pet treat industry by focusing on catnip wine as a luxury pet treat while the remainder of the pet treat market is still focused on chew treats or dry foods. This has allowed Muttley's to be in the prime position of the top luxury pet treat [7].

2. Avoiding Market Saturation:
   Overcrowded markets can diminish profitability and lead to intense competition. By strategically distancing themselves from saturated markets, businesses can find more lucrative opportunities. For instance, Blue Ocean Strategy, a concept introduced by W. Chan Kim and Renée Mauborgne, advocates for creating uncontested market spaces ("blue oceans") rather than competing in saturated markets ("red oceans") [8]. Cirque du Soleil exemplified this by reinventing the circus industry, blending circus arts with theatrical performance to create a new entertainment genre.

3. Partnerships and Alliances:
   Strategic partnerships can help businesses maintain an advantageous distance from competitors. By collaborating with companies that offer complementary strengths, businesses can enhance their capabilities and market reach without directly

confronting rivals. For example, the alliance between Starbucks and Barnes & Noble allowed both companies to leverage each other's customer base and create a unique value proposition that distinguished them from competitors.

A Holistic Approach to Integrating Timing and Distance:

The true power of timing and distance lies in their integration. Businesses that can synchronize their strategic moves with optimal timing and maintain the right distance from competitors, are well-positioned for sustained success.

1. <u>Anticipating and Shaping Market Trends:</u>
   Companies like Amazon have mastered the art of anticipating and shaping market trends by integrating timing and distance into their strategies. Amazon's introduction of Prime membership, which offered faster shipping and exclusive content not only met emerging consumer demands but also created a significant competitive distance. This strategic move was timed perfectly as e-commerce was gaining traction, allowing Amazon to solidify its market dominance.

2. <u>Innovation and Adaptation:</u>
   Innovation requires both timing and distance. Google's acquisition of YouTube in 2006 was a strategic decision that exemplified perfect timing and foresight. Recognizing the burgeoning popularity of online video content, Google acted swiftly to acquire YouTube, distancing itself from other search engines and solidifying its position in the digital advertising space.

3. <u>Strategic Retreats and Advancements:</u>
   Sometimes, maintaining distance involves strategic

retreats. IBM's shift from hardware to services and software in the early 1990s allowed it to distance itself from declining hardware markets and focus on higher-margin, rapidly growing segments. This move, timed during a period of technological transition, enabled IBM to reinvent itself and remain competitive. [9]

Toyota and Lean Manufacturing

Toyota's implementation of lean manufacturing principles, known as the Toyota Production System (TPS), demonstrates the importance of timing and distance in operational strategy. By adopting just-in-time production and continuous improvement practices, Toyota optimized its manufacturing processes and created a significant competitive distance from traditional mass production methods. This strategic approach, timed to capitalize on growing demand for efficient and reliable vehicles, propelled Toyota to global automotive leadership [10].

Procter & Gamble (P&G) and Consumer Insights

P&G's success in consumer goods is largely attributed to its keen sense of timing and understanding of consumer needs. By investing in consumer research and leveraging data analytics, P&G can launch products that align with emerging trends. The introduction of the Swiffer cleaning system, for example, was timed perfectly to address consumer desires for convenient and efficient cleaning solutions, creating a new product category and distancing P&G from competitors [11].

Practical Applications for Businesses

1. Developing a Timing Strategy:
   Businesses should cultivate an acute sense of timing

by closely monitoring market trends, consumer behaviour, and technological advancements. This involves investing in market research, fostering a culture of innovation, and being prepared to act swiftly when opportunities arise. Regularly reviewing and adjusting business strategies to align with current and future trends is crucial for maintaining relevance and competitiveness.

2. <u>Maintaining Strategic Distance:</u>
To maintain strategic distance from competitors, businesses should focus on differentiation and innovation. This can be achieved by: identifying Unique Value Proposition such as developing products or services that offer unique benefits not easily replicated by competitors. Exploring Untapped Markets: Venturing into new or underserved markets where competition is minimal. Building Strong Brand Identity: Establishing a strong brand presence that resonates with consumers and fosters loyalty.

3. <u>Leveraging Technology and Data Analytics:</u>
Advanced technologies and data analytics play a pivotal role in optimizing timing and distance. Businesses should leverage these tools to gain insights into market dynamics, predict consumer preferences, and make data-driven decisions. Implementing AI and machine learning can enhance predictive capabilities, enabling businesses to anticipate trends and respond proactively.

Mastering the concepts of timing and distance, as learned from martial arts, can significantly enhance a business's strategic decision-making process. By understanding the importance of acting at the right moment and maintaining a strategic distance from competitors, businesses can navigate the complexities of the market with agility and precision.

8.

**Redirecting Energy:
Turning Challenges into
Opportunities**

In martial arts, one of the most profound principles is the idea of using an opponent's energy against them. This strategy, prevalent in disciplines such as Judo, Aikido, and Tai Chi, emphasize redirection rather than direct confrontation. By understanding and harnessing the force and momentum of an attacker, martial artists can turn potential threats into opportunities for counterattack. This philosophy translates seamlessly into the business world, where companies often face significant challenges such as economic downturns or aggressive competition. By applying the principle of redirection, businesses can convert these challenges into avenues for growth and success.

Understanding the Principle in Martial Arts

In martial arts, the concept of using an opponent's energy is rooted in efficiency and adaptability. Instead of meeting force with force, students are taught to blend with their opponent's movements, redirecting their energy in a way that neutralizes the threat. This approach minimizes the physical effort required and maximizes effectiveness.

For instance, in Judo, students use techniques such as throws and sweeps that leverage an opponent's momentum. A well-executed throw can send a much larger and stronger opponent to the ground with minimal effort. Similarly, Aikido focuses on circular movements that redirect the opponent's force, turning their aggressive energy into a means of control and balance.

Applying the Principle to Business

Where martial artists use their opponent's energy to gain an advantage, businesses can use external challenges to fuel their growth. This requires a mindset shift from viewing obstacles as threats to seeing them as opportunities. By understanding the dynamics of the market and the nature of the challenges they face, businesses can strategically position themselves to thrive under pressure.

1. Economic Downturns as Catalysts for Innovation: Economic downturns can be devastating, but they also present unique opportunities for innovation and reinvention. Companies that adopt a flexible and adaptive approach can turn financial hardships into a driving force for creativity and efficiency.

   Airbnb During the COVID-19 Pandemic: The COVID-19 pandemic brought the travel industry to a standstill, causing massive disruptions for companies like Airbnb. Instead of succumbing to the downturn, Airbnb pivoted its business model to cater to changing consumer needs. The company introduced "Online Experiences," allowing hosts to offer virtual tours, cooking classes, and other activities. This shift not only helped Airbnb maintain engagement with its user base but also opened up new revenue streams. By leveraging the pandemic's challenges, Airbnb turned a dire situation into an opportunity for growth and diversification [12].

2. Competitive Threats as Opportunities for Differentiation:
Facing intense competition can push businesses to innovate and differentiate themselves. By analysing competitors' strengths and weaknesses, companies can identify gaps in the market and develop unique value propositions. Businesses can also use external challenges to fuel growth which can be compared to martial artists using their opponent's energy and momentum to create an advantage.

Netflix vs. Blockbuster: In the early 2000s, Netflix faced stiff competition from Blockbuster, a dominant player in the video rental market. Instead of directly competing with Blockbuster's brick-and-mortar stores, Netflix leveraged the growing trend of internet usage to introduce a subscription-based DVD rental service by mail. This innovative approach addressed customer pain points such as late fees and limited availability. Eventually, Netflix transitioned to a streaming model, further differentiating itself from traditional rental services. By understanding and redirecting the competitive pressure, Netflix transformed the entertainment industry and emerged as a market leader.

3. <u>Technological Disruptions as Avenues for Transformation:</u>
Technological advancements can disrupt established industries, posing significant challenges to existing businesses. However, these disruptions also offer opportunities for companies to reinvent themselves and stay relevant in a rapidly changing landscape.

IBM's Transition to Cloud Computing: IBM, a pioneer in computing technology, faced declining revenue from its traditional hardware and software businesses in the early 2000s. Recognizing the transformative potential of cloud computing, IBM strategically pivoted its focus toward this emerging technology. They invested heavily in cloud infrastructure and services. This transition not only revitalized the company's growth but also positioned it as a key player in the future of technology. IBM's ability to embrace technological disruption and leverage it for growth exemplifies the martial arts principle of turning challenges into opportunities.

4. <u>Regulatory Changes as Catalysts for Strategic Advantage:</u>
Regulatory changes can create significant hurdles for businesses, but they also offer opportunities for companies that can adapt quickly and strategically.

Tesla and Environmental Regulations: The automotive industry has faced increasing pressure from environmental regulations aimed at reducing carbon emissions. While many traditional automakers struggled to meet these new standards, Tesla embraced the regulatory changes as a strategic advantage. By focusing on electric vehicles (EVs) from the outset, Tesla positioned itself as a leader in sustainable transportation. The company's innovative approach to battery technology, coupled with its early commitment to EVs, allowed it to thrive in a regulatory environment that challenged many of its competitors. Tesla's ability to turn regulatory challenges into a competitive advantage underscores the power of strategic adaptation.

Strategies for Businesses to Turn Challenges into Opportunities

To effectively use the martial arts principle of redirecting energy in business, companies must adopt specific strategies that enable them to adapt and thrive in the face of adversity.

1. Embrace Agility and Flexibility: Businesses must be agile and flexible to respond quickly to changing circumstances. This requires a culture that encourages innovation, experimentation, and adaptability. Companies should invest in continuous learning and development to ensure their teams are equipped to handle new challenges.

2. Leverage Data and Insights: Understanding the market and competitive landscape is crucial for turning challenges into opportunities. Businesses should leverage data and analytics to gain insights into customer behaviour, market trends, and competitive dynamics. This information can inform strategic decisions and help companies identify opportunities for differentiation and growth.

3. Foster a Resilient Mindset: A resilient mindset is essential for navigating adversity. Businesses should cultivate a culture that views challenges as opportunities for growth rather than threats. This involves encouraging a positive attitude, resilience, and perseverance among employees. Leaders should communicate a clear vision and inspire their teams to stay focused and motivated, even in difficult times.

4. Invest in Innovation and R&D: Innovation is a key driver of growth in challenging times. Businesses should invest in research and development (R&D) to explore new technologies, products, and business models. This investment can lead to breakthrough innovations that position the company for long-term success.

5. Build Strategic Partnerships: Collaborating with other businesses, organizations, or industry experts can provide valuable insights and resources. Strategic partnerships can help companies access new markets, technologies, and capabilities. By working together, businesses can overcome challenges more effectively and seize new opportunities.

6. Enhance Customer Focus: Understanding and addressing customer needs is crucial during challenging times. Businesses should prioritize customer feedback and adapt their offerings to meet changing demands. By staying close to their customers, companies can build loyalty and drive growth, even in adverse conditions.

The principle of using an opponent's energy against them in martial arts offers valuable insights for businesses facing challenges. By embracing agility, leveraging data, fostering resilience, investing in innovation, building strategic partnerships, and enhancing customer focus, companies can turn adversity into opportunity. The examples of Airbnb, Netflix, IBM, and Tesla demonstrate that with the right mindset and strategies, businesses can thrive even in the most challenging environments. By applying the martial arts philosophy of sabaki, businesses can not only survive but also achieve remarkable growth and success.

9.

Anticipation and Adaptation: Staying Ahead in a Competitive Market

Anticipation is a skill that can mean the difference between success and failure. In martial arts, it involves reading an opponent's movements and intentions to counteract or pre-empt their actions. Similarly, in business, anticipation involves staying ahead of market trends, foreseeing potential challenges, and adapting swiftly to new developments.

This chapter will delve into the importance of anticipation, explore strategies for staying ahead, and provide examples of companies that have thrived by being proactive rather than reactive.

The Role of Anticipation in Martial Arts

Anticipation in martial arts is about understanding and predicting an opponent's next move. This skill is cultivated through rigorous training and a deep understanding of human behaviour and techniques.

Observation and Analysis:
Martial artists spend countless hours observing their opponents by studying their habits, and analysing their strategies prior to a fight. This process enables them to anticipate attacks and respond effectively.

Pattern Recognition:
Through experience, martial artists learn to recognize patterns in their opponents' behaviour. This ability allows them to predict and counteract moves before they fully unfold.

Mental Preparation:
Anticipation also involves mental readiness. Martial artists train their minds to remain calm and focused, enabling them to react swiftly and accurately under pressure.

Strategies for Staying Ahead in Business

In business, anticipation translates strategic foresight into market intelligence, and adaptability. Companies that excel in anticipation are often those that lead their industries and set trends rather than follow them. Here are key strategies for staying ahead:

Market Research and Trend Analysis:

1. Conduct regular market research to stay informed about industry trends, consumer preferences, and emerging technologies.

2. Use data analytics to identify patterns and predict future market movements.

3. Monitor competitors to understand their strategies and anticipate their next moves.

Innovation and Continuous Improvement:

1. Foster a culture of innovation within the organization by encouraging employees to think creatively and propose new ideas.

2. Invest in research and development to stay at the forefront of technological advancements.

3. Continuously improve products and services based on customer feedback and market demands.

Agility and Flexibility:

1. Develop agile business processes that allow for rapid adaptation to changing circumstances.

2. Create cross-functional teams that can respond quickly to new opportunities or threats.

3. Embrace a flexible mindset that encourages experimentation and learning from failures.

Customer Engagement and Feedback:

1. Maintain strong relationships with customers to understand their needs and preferences, whilst using their feedback to drive product development and service improvements.

2. Anticipate changes in customer behaviour by staying attuned to societal trends and shifts.

Companies that are thriving through proactive strategies:

Several companies have demonstrated the power of anticipation by proactively staying ahead of market trends and adapting to new developments. Here are a few notable examples:

Apple:

1. Innovation: Apple has consistently led the market with innovative products like the iPhone, iPad, and Apple Watch. By anticipating consumer desires for sleek, user-friendly devices, Apple has set industry standards.

2. Adaptability: Apple continually adapts to technological advancements and consumer preferences. The introduction of services like Apple Music and Apple TV+ showcases their ability to diversify and stay relevant.

Amazon:

1. Customer-Centric Approach: Amazon's focus on customer satisfaction has driven its success. By anticipating the need for faster delivery, Amazon introduced Prime, revolutionizing the e-commerce industry.

2. Technological Advancements: Amazon's investment in AI and machine learning has enabled them to predict customer preferences and optimize supply chain operations.

Tesla:

1. Forward Thinking Leadership: Elon Musk's vision for sustainable energy and electric vehicles has positioned Tesla as a leader in the automotive industry. Tesla anticipated the shift towards environmentally friendly transportation long before it became mainstream.

2. Continuous Innovation: Tesla's focus on innovation, from self-driving technology to energy storage solutions, has kept them ahead of competitors.

Nike:

3. Customer Engagement: Nike engages with customers through various touchpoints, from social media to in-store experiences. By listening to their customers, Nike can anticipate trends and develop products that resonate.

4. Technological Integration: Nike's investment in technology, such as the Nike Training Club app and Nike Adapt self-lacing shoes, showcases their ability to anticipate and leverage technological advancements.

Some proactive strategies aren't always at the best interests of staff and communities. In martial arts every act of violence is done to protect yourself or protect others from physical harm. This isn't always the case in business and while it is important to continue to progress and succeed, it is also important to consider all implications of your strategy to ensure you aren't marginalising or negatively affecting different social communities or at worst harming people.

Building a Proactive Business Culture

To foster a culture of anticipation, businesses must prioritize certain values and practices:

Encourage Curiosity and Learning:
Promote a culture of curiosity where employees are encouraged to explore new ideas and learn continuously. This can be achieved through training programs, workshops, and access to educational resources.

Embrace Change:
Encourage a mindset that views change as an opportunity rather than a threat. This involves being open to new ideas, adapting to market shifts, and embracing technological advancements.

Foster Collaboration:
Collaboration across departments can lead to innovative solutions and proactive strategies. Encourage cross-functional teams to work together on projects and share insights.

Invest in Technology:
Invest in technology and tools that enable data analysis, market research, and competitive intelligence. These tools can provide valuable insights that drive proactive decision-making.

Develop Strategic Foresight:
Implement strategic foresight practices, such as scenario planning and forecasting, to anticipate future market developments. This involves considering various potential futures and preparing for different outcomes.

The Intersection of Martial Arts and Business

The principles of anticipation in martial arts can be directly applied to business strategies. Both disciplines require a deep understanding of opponents (competitors), the ability to recognize patterns, and the mental agility to adapt swiftly.

Reading the Competition:

1. Where martial artists study their opponents, businesses must also keep a close eye on competitors. This involves analysing competitors' strengths, weaknesses, and strategies to anticipate their next moves.
2. Competitive intelligence tools can provide valuable insights into market positioning and potential threats.

Recognizing Market Patterns:

1. Businesses, like martial artists, must recognize and respond to patterns. This could involve identifying seasonal trends, economic cycles, or shifts in consumer behaviour.
2. Data analytics and machine learning can aid in recognizing and predicting these patterns, allowing businesses to make informed decisions.

Maintaining Mental Agility:

1. In martial arts, mental agility is crucial for reacting to unexpected moves. Similarly, businesses need to foster a culture of agility and flexibility.
2. This can be achieved by empowering employees to make quick decisions, encouraging innovation, and being open to change.

Anticipation is a critical skill in both martial arts and business. In martial arts, it involves reading an opponent's moves and responding effectively. In business, it means staying ahead of market trends, anticipating challenges, and adapting swiftly to new developments.

By adopting strategies such as rigorous market research, creative strategies, fostering innovation, and maintaining agility, businesses can thrive in a constantly changing environment.

The success stories of companies like Apple, Amazon, Tesla, and Netflix highlight the power of proactive strategies. These companies have demonstrated that by anticipating market trends and adapting to new developments, they can lead their industries and set benchmarks for others to follow.

Ultimately, the principles of anticipation in martial arts offer valuable lessons for businesses. By reading the competition, recognizing market patterns, and maintaining mental agility, businesses can navigate challenges and seize opportunities.

10.

Counter-Strategy: Defending Against Competitor Moves

In martial arts, countering an opponent's moves successfully is a fundamental skill that can mean the difference between victory and defeat. This principle of countering, where a practitioner not only defends against an attack but uses it to their advantage, is as applicable in business as it is in the dojo. In business, companies must constantly defend their market position and respond to competitor initiatives with strategic finesse. The concept of countering in martial arts and how it translates to effective business strategy is key to the corporate sabaki method so in the following pages we will look into the defensive strategies that businesses can use, along with case studies of companies that have successfully used counter-strategies to maintain or enhance their market position.

Understanding the Art of Countering in Martial Arts

In martial arts, countering involves anticipating an opponent's move and responding in a way that neutralizes the attack and puts the defender in a favourable position to attack from. There are many key components to effective countering including:

Anticipation and Timing: Recognizing the opponent's intent before they fully commit to their move.

Positioning: Placing oneself in a location that maximizes defence and allows for a swift counterattack.

Utilization of Force: Redirecting the opponent's energy and momentum to one's advantage.

Adaptability: Being flexible and responsive to changing situations and tactics.

Translating Countering Principles to Business Strategy

In the business world, countering involves recognizing competitive threats and responding in a way that protects the company's market position while potentially gaining an advantage. The principles of anticipation, positioning, utilization of resources, and adaptability are equally important. Below we explore how these principles manifest in business strategies.

Anticipation and Timing:
In business, anticipating a competitor's moves requires thorough market analysis and competitive intelligence. Companies must stay vigilant, monitoring industry trends, consumer behavior, and competitor activities. Timely

responses are crucial, as delayed reactions can result in lost market share.

Apple and Samsung have long been rivals in the smartphone market. Apple, known for its innovative products, has often led the market with groundbreaking technology. However, Samsung has been adept at anticipating Apple's moves and timing its responses. For instance, when Apple launched the iPhone with a large touchscreen, Samsung quickly followed with its Galaxy series, offering similar features at competitive prices. Samsung's ability to anticipate Apple's innovations and time its product launches effectively has allowed it to maintain a strong market presence.

Positioning:
Positioning in business involves strategic placement in the market to maximize competitive advantage. This includes targeting specific customer segments, differentiating products, and creating a strong brand identity.

Coca-Cola and Pepsi have been engaged in a long-standing battle for dominance in the soft drink market. Coca-Cola's strategic positioning has been a key factor in maintaining its market leadership. By focusing on global branding, emotional marketing, and a strong distribution network, Coca-Cola has positioned itself as a timeless and universal brand. Pepsi, on the other hand, has positioned itself as the choice for the younger generation, often leveraging pop culture and celebrity endorsements. Both companies have used strategic positioning to counter each other's market moves effectively.

Utilization of Resources:
In business, utilizing resources effectively involves leveraging strengths, such as brand equity, technology, and human capital, to counteract competitive threats.

Adaptability:
Adaptability in business means being flexible and responsive to market changes and competitor actions. Companies that can pivot their strategies and innovate are better positioned to counter competitive threats.

Microsoft's adaptability has been evident in its response to Google's dominance in the search engine and online advertising markets. Initially slow to react, Microsoft eventually launched Bing, a direct competitor to Google Search. More importantly, Microsoft shifted its focus to cloud computing, recognizing the growing demand for cloud services. By investing heavily in Azure, its cloud platform, Microsoft adapted to market trends and countered Google's influence in the tech industry. This adaptability has allowed Microsoft to remain competitive and relevant in a rapidly evolving market.

Defensive Strategies for Business

To effectively counter competitor initiatives, businesses can employ a variety of defensive strategies. These strategies are designed to protect market position, mitigate risks, and turn potential threats into opportunities.

Market Fortification:
Market fortification involves strengthening the company's position in its existing markets. This can be achieved through brand loyalty programs, improving product quality, and enhancing customer service.

Starbucks has fortified its market position by creating a strong brand identity and fostering customer loyalty. Through initiatives like the Starbucks Rewards program, the company has built a dedicated customer base. Additionally, Starbucks continuously innovates its product offerings and focuses on delivering a high-quality customer experience. These efforts have helped Starbucks maintain its market leadership despite increasing competition from other coffee chains and independent cafes.

Diversification:
Diversification involves expanding the company's product or service offerings to reduce dependence on a single market. This strategy can help mitigate risks and provide alternative revenue streams.

Amazon's diversification strategy has been a cornerstone of its success. Initially an online bookstore, Amazon expanded its offerings to include electronics, clothing, and eventually became a global e-commerce giant. Additionally, Amazon ventured into cloud computing with AWS, media with Amazon Prime Video, and even grocery retail with the acquisition of Whole Foods. By diversifying its business, Amazon has reduced its vulnerability to market fluctuations and competitive pressures in any single sector whilst creating a powerhouse that begins to dominate any industry it enters.

Strategic Alliances:
Forming strategic alliances with other companies can enhance a business's competitive position and provide access to new markets, technologies, and expertise.

Spotify and Uber formed a strategic alliance that allowed Uber riders to stream their favourite music during rides. This partnership benefited both companies by enhancing the customer experience and creating cross-promotional opportunities. For Spotify, it provided exposure to a broader audience, while Uber differentiated its service by offering a unique in-car entertainment option. Strategic alliances like this can help companies counter competitive threats by leveraging each other's strengths.

Innovation and R&D:
Investing in research and development (R&D) to drive innovation is a critical defensive strategy. Companies that continually innovate are better equipped to counteract competitor initiatives and meet changing customer needs.

Case Studies of Successful Counter-Strategies

To illustrate how businesses have successfully employed counter-strategies, let's examine a few detailed case studies.

Case Study 1: IBM vs. Competitors in the Technology Sector

Background: IBM, a pioneer in the technology industry, faced significant competition from emerging tech companies in the 1990s and 2000s. Companies like Microsoft, Oracle, and later Google and Amazon, began to dominate various segments of the technology market.

Counter-Strategy: IBM employed a combination of market fortification, diversification, and strategic alliances to counter these competitive threats. Recognizing the shift towards cloud computing and AI, IBM invested heavily in these areas. The acquisition of Red Hat, a leading provider of open-source software solutions, bolstered IBM's cloud offerings and allowed it to compete more effectively with Amazon Web Services and Microsoft Azure.

Outcome: By diversifying its portfolio and forming strategic alliances, IBM repositioned itself as a leader in hybrid cloud and AI technologies. This strategic pivot allowed IBM to counteract the dominance of its competitors and maintain a strong presence in the technology sector.

Case Study 2: McDonald's vs. Health-Conscious Trends

Background: In the early 2000s, McDonald's faced increasing competition from health-conscious consumers and the rise of fast-casual dining options like Chipotle and Panera Bread. These competitors offered healthier menu options and positioned themselves as more wholesome alternatives to traditional fast food.

Counter-Strategy: McDonald's responded by implementing a series of defensive strategies. The company revamped its menu to include healthier options, such as salads, fruit, and low-calorie meals. McDonald's also improved transparency by providing nutritional information and sourcing sustainable ingredients. Additionally, the company invested in modernizing its restaurants to enhance the customer experience.

Outcome: These strategic moves helped McDonald's counter the health-conscious trend and regain its market position. By adapting to changing consumer preferences and improving its offerings, McDonald's successfully mitigated the competitive threat posed by fast-casual restaurants.

Case Study 3: Netflix vs. Disney+

Background: The launch of Disney+ in 2019 posed a significant threat to Netflix's dominance in the streaming industry. Disney's extensive library of content, including popular franchises like Star Wars and Marvel, attracted millions of subscribers and challenged Netflix's market leadership.

Counter-Strategy: Netflix responded by doubling down on original content production and securing exclusive deals with top creators. The company invested billions in developing a diverse range of original shows and movies to differentiate itself from Disney+. Netflix also expanded its global reach by producing content tailored to international markets.

Outcome: Netflix's focus on original content and global expansion helped it to consolidate its position as a top streaming service, whilst also ensuring that unique content gave their subscribers a strong reason to stay with their service. Netflix has also leaned into social media sites as a key way to drive traffic and interest to their site. They produce such massive amounts of content that you can find a show on almost any subject. This means that people are more likely to use Netflix as the base subscription and then get additional streaming services on a temporary basis when they want to watch something specific that isn't on Netflix.

Counter manoeuvre strategies are a vital thing to have in your arsenal as a business leader, with the main counter strategies including anticipation and timing, positioning, utilisation of forces and adaptability; through mastering these you will be able to swiftly understand which method will work best for the situation that you find yourself in.

The utilisation of defensive strategies is equally important to the counter manoeuvres as it gives you a strategy to use if your opponent decides to use a counter move against you. Business can be like chess where you always need to be thinking multiple steps ahead, this is where the defensive strategies come in as you can plan your defensive strategies in advance if you understand what your opponent will do in reaction to your attack.

The defensive strategies that work most effectively for Small to medium sized businesses (SME's) is diversification as you are able to balance your loss of revenue risks by being in different market segments; the other useful defensive strategy for SME's is strategic alliances. This is because it gives you the ability to leverage the more powerful brand's image that you are partnering with.

The defensive strategies that usually work best for larger corporations are utilisation of resources, this is because you already have vast resources and by adjusting them more effectively or in a more focused manner you can generally smash down your smaller opponent. This is if they don't use a sabaki method against you by attacking a blind spot. The other strategy that works well for larger businesses is market fortification, if you are being attacked by guerrilla tactics or eclectic types of attacks then fortifying your market can work. This is because although the opponent can start attacking different areas to usual or having short bursts of heavy attacking, through fortifying your position as the market leader you can wait out the guerilla tactics which are trying to smash you quickly. You can usually do this because of a limited budget or limited resources by the attacking opponent, if you can successfully defend yourself the attacking should decrease.

As the market leader and a larger corporation, the perfect complement to the market fortification tactic is the Innovation and R&D strategy. This is because while you are fortifying your market from attacks you have the ability to pull your resources together and assess what the opponent is doing and then sabaki them with an attack to their fortifying pillar. You do this by pulling to market a new patented product that makes your opponent obsolete.

These strategic examples above are how you practically use the methodology in this chapter to help defend and grow your business.

11.

Controlled Aggression: Knowing When to Strike in Business

Controlled aggression in martial arts is the skilful use of force, tempered with strategy and precision. It's not about acting on impulse or sheer brute strength, but about harnessing energy and aggression to strike at the opportune moment. This concept is integral to various martial arts disciplines, where practitioners learn to balance offensive and defensive techniques, waiting for the perfect moment to act decisively.

Key Principles of Controlled Aggression

Timing:
Martial artists must develop an acute sense of timing. This involves not only knowing when to attack but also understanding when to hold back. A premature move can expose vulnerabilities, while a delayed action might miss the opportunity.

Precision:
Aggression in martial arts is not wild or uncontrolled. Each strike, block, or movement is calculated to maximize the impact and efficiency. Precision ensures that energy is not wasted and that each action serves a strategic purpose.

Self-Control:
Mastery of controlled aggression requires immense self-discipline. Martial artists train to manage their emotions and maintain composure, even under pressure. This mental fortitude is crucial for making clear-headed decisions.

Anticipation:
Anticipating an opponent's moves allows martial artists to prepare their response. This foresight comes from keen observation and understanding of the opponent's patterns and behaviours.

Real-World Martial Arts Example: Bruce Lee's Jeet Kune Do

Bruce Lee's Jeet Kune Do embodies the essence of controlled aggression. Lee emphasized the importance of intercepting an opponent's attack and using their momentum against them. He taught that the best defence is a well-timed offense, delivered with precision and minimal effort. This approach allows practitioners to maintain control and assert dominance in a confrontation.

Translating Controlled Aggression into Business

In the business world, controlled aggression translates to strategic assertiveness. Businesses must balance patience with action, timing their moves to maximize impact. This is similar to martial arts where both involve understanding market dynamics, anticipating competitor actions, tempering when to attack hard or distract and seizing opportunities with calculated precision.

Key Principles of Controlled Aggression in Business

1. Strategic Timing: Businesses must identify the right moments to launch new products or enter new markets to help them execute bold new initiatives. This timing can be influenced by market conditions, political conditions, consumer trends, and competitor actions.

2. Calculated Risks: Just as martial artists strike with precision; businesses must take calculated risks. This involves thorough analysis and planning to ensure that actions are not hasty or reckless.

3. Resource Management: Efficient use of resources—whether financial, human, or technological—is essential. Controlled aggression in business means deploying resources where they can have the most significant impact.

4. Competitive Intelligence: Anticipating competitors' moves allows businesses to stay ahead. This requires ongoing market analysis and a deep understanding of competitors' strategies and weaknesses.

Strategic Business Initiatives Leveraging Controlled Aggression

Standard Oil
The story of standard oil is a perfect example of controlled aggression. Standard oil was the company run and owned by John D. Rockefeller which denominated the oil market through monopolising the production, processing, marketing and transportation. The company managed to create this position through mergers and forcing opposition out of the market with favourable railroad rebates for their oil making it cheaper and consolidating operations to make it more efficient. They also created a maze of legal structures to make it near impossible for governments and authorities to understand how the business operated [13]. This model is now outlawed due to anti-monopoly legislation that was brought in as a result of standard oil and other robber barons.

Although this tactic of controlled aggression is no longer able to be used in most countries it is an important one to study. You can use a toned-down version of this where acquisitions of different brands selling in the same industry can be used to flood the market if the business has a strong distribution network, while you expand outside of the original market to diversify the risk of a forced sell off of a brand. If a forced sell down is required then you sell off the weaker brand and create another new one to replace its space in your portfolio with a small adjustment to either the marketing or positioning to begin your build back to majority again.

Cadbury
Cadbury during WWII managed to gain a key war contract for their chocolate and they created a price fight which severely

injured J.S. Fry and sons, Cadbury began ploughing football fields after parts of their Bourneville factory were turned into milling spaces to produce seats for fighter pilots. Through a streamlining of operations and strong marketing campaigns they were able to take a large section of the chocolate industry in Europe. This put J.S. Fry and sons in a position where they had to rebuild their product range as they simply could no longer compete with Cadbury's dairy milk with their alternative [14]. This was a text book example of controlled aggression where you push the price down to the point competitors can no longer withstand to be in the market through a simplification and streamlining of operations.

The key way to defend against this is a sabaki movement where you attack somewhere new - Fry's did this by consolidating their range of random low selling product lines down and pushing products such as Turkish Delight and creating the honey comb Crunchie bar. Cadbury had no answer to the Crunchie Bar due to it's complicated manufacturing method and unusual size. The streamlined operations of Cadbury were not able to handle more creative products [15]. As a result of this, consumers began to move away from dairy milk chocolate for a new flavour and Fry's began to gain market share back from Cadbury. Cadbury then merged with Fry's to help bolster its own poor financial situation that was caused by a decrease in revenue and a low profit product [16].

Applying Controlled Aggression in Business Strategy

To effectively implement controlled aggression in business, organizations can follow a structured approach:

1. Market Analysis and Research: Comprehensive market research is the foundation of strategic

assertiveness. Understanding market trends, customer needs, and competitor strategies provides the insights needed to make informed decisions.

2. Scenario Planning: Businesses should develop multiple scenarios based on different market conditions. This allows for flexibility and adaptability, ensuring that the organization is prepared for various outcomes.

3. Strategic Planning: Clear, actionable plans are vitally important. This includes setting specific goals, identifying key performance indicators (KPIs), and outlining the steps needed to achieve these objectives.

4. Risk Management: Identifying potential risks and developing mitigation strategies is crucial. Controlled aggression involves taking risks, but these risks should be calculated and managed effectively.

5. Continuous Monitoring and Adjustment: The business landscape is dynamic, and strategies must evolve accordingly. Continuous monitoring of market conditions and competitor actions allows businesses to adjust their plans and stay ahead.

Balancing Patience and Assertiveness

One of the critical challenges in applying controlled aggression is finding the right balance between patience and assertiveness. Businesses must avoid the pitfalls of acting too hastily or waiting too long. Here are some strategies to strike this balance:

1. Data-Driven Decision Making: Relying on data and analytics helps reduce uncertainty and provides a solid basis for decision-making. This approach

ensures that actions are not based on intuition alone but are supported by empirical evidence.

2. <u>Agility and Flexibility:</u> Building an agile organization allows businesses to respond quickly to changing market conditions. This involves fostering a culture of innovation and continuous improvement, where teams are empowered to adapt and pivot as needed.

3. <u>Incremental Aggression:</u> Rather than making a single bold move, businesses can adopt a strategy of incremental aggression. This involves taking smaller, calculated steps that build momentum over time. This approach allows for course corrections and reduces the risk of significant setbacks.

4. <u>Stakeholder Engagement</u>: Engaging with stakeholders—employees, customers, partners, and investors—provides valuable insights and helps build support for strategic initiatives. Collaborative decision-making ensures that diverse perspectives are considered, reducing the risk of blind spots.

Controlled aggression in martial arts and business requires a delicate balance of timing, precision, and strategic insight. Martial artists learn to strike at the opportune moment, businesses must identify the right times to assert themselves in the market. By leveraging principles of controlled aggression, companies can navigate competitive landscapes, seize opportunities, and achieve sustained success.

The examples of Standard Oil and Cadbury illustrate how strategic assertiveness can drive market domination but the use of a sabaki strategy by J.S. Fry and Sons shows how an effective strategy can take down even the most dominating businesses.

Ultimately, controlled aggression is about harnessing the power of action and restraint, ensuring that every move is purposeful and impactful. Whether in the dojo or the boardroom, mastering this balance is key to achieving excellence and overcoming challenges.

12.

Finding the Opening: Identifying and Exploiting Market Gaps

The ability to identify and capitalize on openings is a critical skill that can determine success or failure. In martial arts, this skill involves recognizing moments of vulnerability in an opponent and exploiting them to gain an advantage. In business, it translates to identifying market gaps or unmet customer needs and addressing them effectively. Let's look into the parallels between these two disciplines, exploring methods for discovering market gaps and providing case studies of businesses that have successfully capitalized on these opportunities.

Finding Openings in Martial Arts

In martial arts, finding openings is a combination of strategic thinking, keen observation, and precise execution of strikes. Students are trained to anticipate their opponent's moves, recognize patterns, and exploit weaknesses. This requires a deep understanding of techniques, timing, and positioning. The key principles include:

Observation and Awareness:
Constantly observing the opponent's movements, anticipating their actions, and identifying moments when they are off-balance or exposed.

Timing and Speed:
Executing techniques with perfect timing and speed to exploit the opponent's vulnerabilities effectively.

Positioning:
Maintaining optimal distance and angles to create opportunities for attack while minimizing exposure to counterattacks.

Adaptability:
Being flexible and adaptive to changes in the opponent's strategy, quickly adjusting tactics to seize openings.

Identifying Market Gaps in Business

Similarly, in business, identifying market gaps involves recognizing unmet needs or underserved markets. This process requires:

Market Research and Analysis:
Conducting comprehensive market research to understand consumer trends and the competitive landscape.

Customer Feedback and Insights:
Gathering and analysing customer feedback to identify pain points, preferences, and unmet needs.

SWOT Analysis:
Performing SWOT (Strengths, Weaknesses, Opportunities, Threats) analysis to uncover areas where competitors are lacking and opportunities for differentiation.

Innovation and Creativity:
Leveraging creativity and innovation to develop unique solutions that address identified gaps and meet customer needs effectively.

Agility and Responsiveness:
Being agile and responsive to market changes, quickly adapting strategies to capitalize on emerging opportunities.

Business examples that capitalized on market gaps

Muttley's Estate – Pet wine
Identifying the Gap: When researching new pet products to manufacture, Muttley's estate searched the global markets to see where new brands and new innovations were coming through. There was the emergence of dog beers but nothing that looks after cats as well as dogs. Searching through relevant websites and stores the amount of cat treats was minimal other than general cat food or play toys. This is where the thought to launch a catnip wine came in.

Strategy and Execution: Muttley's Estate now had the perfect product to take to market but it didn't have a strong distribution network. The easiest way to achieve this was to work with a local distributor to help get retail locations quickly. This worked and within the first week of launch there were 20 retail locations stocking the products. From here the next step was to build the brand position and get the name known, this is where social media and influencers came into play.

Outcome: By addressing the market gap in luxury pet treats they were able to own the space as the top pet wine, eventually winning a global award for top pet wine. With the introduction of Muttley's Estate pet wine there have now been others come into the market but Muttley's strong position early on cemented its position as the industry leader.

Airbnb: Revolutionizing the Hospitality Industry
Identifying the Gap: Traditional hotel accommodations were often expensive and lacked the personalized experience that many travellers sought. There was a growing demand for more affordable and unique accommodation options.

Strategy and Execution: Airbnb identified this gap and created a platform that allowed homeowners to rent out their properties to travellers. This not only provided a more personalized and affordable option for travellers but also created a new source of income for property owners.

Outcome: By tapping into the sharing economy and addressing the unmet needs of both travellers and property owners, Airbnb rapidly grew and became a major player in the hospitality industry, challenging traditional hotel chains.

Methods for Discovering Market Gaps

Conducting Market Research and Analysis
Market research is the foundation for identifying gaps in the market. Businesses can use various methods to gather data, including surveys, focus groups, and competitive analysis.

Tools like Google Trends, market reports, and customer feedback platforms provide valuable insights into emerging trends and consumer behaviour.

Procter & Gamble (P&G) is known for its rigorous market research. Before launching a new product, P&G conducts extensive consumer research to understand their needs and preferences. This approach has led to successful product innovations such as the Swiffer cleaning system and Tide Pods, which addressed specific customer pain points.

Analysing Customer Feedback and Insights
Listening to customers and analysing their feedback helps businesses understand their pain points, preferences, and unmet needs. This can be done through direct feedback channels, social media monitoring, and customer reviews.

Apple's success is partly attributed to its focus on customer feedback. The company continually gathers and analyses user feedback to improve its products and services. For instance, customer feedback played a crucial role in the development of features like Face ID and the redesign of the MacBook keyboard.

Performing SWOT Analysis
SWOT analysis helps businesses identify their strengths, weaknesses, opportunities, and threats. By understanding their competitive position and the external environment, businesses can uncover market gaps and opportunities for growth.

A startup in the health and wellness industry might perform a SWOT analysis and discover that while there are many fitness apps, few focus on mental health and holistic wellness. This insight could lead to the development of an app that integrates physical fitness, mental health, and nutrition, filling a gap in the market.

Leveraging Innovation and Creativity
Innovation and creativity are crucial for identifying and addressing market gaps. Businesses should foster a culture of innovation, encouraging employees to think creatively and explore new ideas.

Being Agile and Responsive
In today's fast-paced business environment, agility and responsiveness are essential for capitalizing on market opportunities. Businesses should be prepared to pivot and adapt their strategies based on market changes and emerging trends.

During the COVID-19 pandemic, many companies had to quickly adapt to the changing market conditions. For instance, distilleries like Bacardi and Pernod Ricard pivoted their production to create hand sanitizers, addressing the sudden surge in demand and helping to fill a critical gap in the market.

Applying Martial Arts Strategies to Business
The principles of finding openings in martial arts can be directly applied to business strategies for identifying market gaps:

Observation and Awareness:
Similar to how martial artists observe their opponents, businesses must observe the market. Their competitors and customers behaviour will signify where to identify opportunities by either feedback supplied by customers or competitors beginning to enter new segments of the market. It is important to stay informed about industry trends,

competitor activities, new product introductions and actively seeking customer feedback.

Timing and Speed:
In martial arts, the right timing can turn the tide of a match. Similarly, businesses must act swiftly to seize market opportunities. Being the first to market with a new product or service can provide a significant competitive advantage.

Positioning:
Effective positioning involves creating a unique value proposition that differentiates the business from competitors. This can be achieved by addressing specific customer needs that are currently unmet or underserved.

Adaptability:
The ability to adapt to changing market conditions is crucial. Businesses that are flexible and responsive to customer needs and market trends are more likely to identify and capitalize on new opportunities.

The skills of finding openings in martial arts and identifying market gaps in business share many similarities. Both require focused observation, strategic thinking, precise execution, and the ability to adapt to changing conditions. By applying these principles, businesses can uncover unmet customer needs and underserved markets, developing innovative solutions that drive growth and success. The case studies of Muttley's Estate and Airbnb demonstrate how identifying and addressing market gaps can lead to significant industry disruption and market leadership. By conducting thorough market research, analysing customer feedback, performing SWOT analysis, fostering innovation, and maintaining agility, businesses can effectively identify and capitalize on market opportunities, achieving sustained success in today's competitive landscape.

13.

Balance and Stability: Maintaining a Strong Business Foundation

Maintaining a strong business foundation is key to the balance and stability of your company, this is why they are fundamental principles that underpin your success. Just as a martial artist must maintain a strong, stable stance to execute techniques effectively and avoid being overpowered by an opponent, a business must establish a solid foundation to thrive and grow sustainably. This chapter will explore the importance of balance and stability in martial arts and business, offering strategies for managing resources, maintaining a strong organizational culture, and ensuring financial stability.

Balance and Stability in Martial Arts

In martial arts, balance and stability are essential for both offense and defence. A well-balanced stance provides the foundation from which a martial artist can generate power, move quickly, and respond to an opponent's actions. Key principles include:

Centre of Gravity:
A martial artist must keep their centre of gravity low and within their base of support to maintain balance. This principle ensures stability and allows for swift, controlled movements.

Rooting:
This concept involves establishing a firm connection with the ground, creating a sense of being "rooted." Rooting enhances stability and allows the martial artist to withstand and absorb external forces.

Posture and Alignment:
Proper posture and body alignment are crucial for maintaining balance. An upright posture with aligned joints ensures efficient movement and minimizes the risk of injury.

Dynamic Balance:
Martial artists must maintain balance not only when stationary but also during movement. This dynamic balance allows for fluid transitions between techniques and effective responses to an opponent's attacks.

Balance and Stability in Business

In the business world, balance and stability are equally vital. Companies must balance various aspects of their operations to achieve long-term success and growth. Key areas include:

Financial Stability:
Ensuring financial stability is crucial for a business's survival

and growth. This involves managing cash flow, maintaining healthy profit margins, and building reserves for unforeseen challenges. As this is the centre of gravity for most businesses it is a key area to protect as a sure-fire way to crumble an opponent quickly is to attack their centre of gravity.

Organizational Culture:
A strong, positive organizational culture fosters stability by promoting employee engagement, loyalty, positivity and productivity. Companies with a solid culture are better equipped to navigate challenges and adapt to change.

Strategic Planning:
Strategic planning involves setting clear goals and developing actionable plans to achieve them. Businesses must balance short-term objectives with long-term vision to ensure sustainable growth.

Resource Management:
Effective resource management involves optimizing the use of financial, human, and material resources. Businesses must allocate resources wisely to support growth while avoiding waste and inefficiencies.

Strategies for Maintaining Balance and Stability in Business

Effective Resource Management

Managing resources efficiently is critical for maintaining balance and stability. This involves optimizing the use of financial, human, and material resources to support growth and sustainability.

Financial Resources:

- Budgeting and Forecasting: Implement robust budgeting and forecasting processes to ensure accurate financial planning and resource allocation.

- Cost Control: Monitor and control expenses to maintain healthy profit margins. Identify areas where costs can be reduced without compromising quality.

- Diversified Revenue Streams: Develop multiple revenue streams to reduce dependency on a single source. This diversification can enhance financial stability and mitigate risks.

Human Resources:

- Talent Management: Attract, develop, and retain top talent to build a skilled and motivated workforce. Invest in employee training and development to enhance skills and productivity.

- Workforce Planning: Align workforce planning with business goals to ensure the right talent is in place to support growth. Consider both current and future staffing needs.

- **Employee Engagement:** Foster a positive work environment that promotes engagement and loyalty. Recognize and reward employee contributions to enhance morale and productivity.

Material Resources:

- **Inventory Management:** Implement efficient inventory management practices to optimize stock levels and reduce waste. Use technology to track and manage inventory in real-time.

- **Supply Chain Optimization:** Streamline supply chain processes to improve efficiency and reduce costs. Build strong relationships with suppliers to ensure reliable access to materials.

- **Sustainable Practices:** Adopt sustainable practices to minimize environmental impact and enhance operational efficiency. This can also improve the company's reputation and appeal to eco-conscious consumers.

Maintaining a Strong Organizational Culture

A strong organizational culture is a key driver of stability and success. It fosters employee engagement, loyalty, and productivity, creating a resilient and adaptable workforce.

Core Values and Vision:

- **Define Core Values:** Clearly define and communicate the company's core values and vision. Ensure these values are integrated into all aspects of the business, from hiring practices to decision-making processes.

- **Leadership Alignment:** Ensure leadership is aligned with the company's values and vision. Leaders should model these values and inspire employees to do the same.

- Cultural Fit: Hire employees who align with the company's culture and values. This ensures a cohesive and harmonious work environment.

Employee Engagement:

- Open Communication: Foster open and transparent communication between employees and leadership. Encourage feedback and create channels for employees to voice their ideas and concerns.

- Recognition and Rewards: Recognize and reward employee contributions to enhance morale and motivation. Implement formal recognition programs and celebrate achievements.

- Work-Life Balance: Promote work-life balance by offering flexible work arrangements and support for employee well-being. This can reduce stress and enhance job satisfaction.

Diversity and Inclusion:

- Inclusive Practices: Implement inclusive practices that promote diversity and equal opportunities. Create a work environment where all employees feel valued and respected.

- Training and Awareness: Provide training on diversity and inclusion to raise awareness and promote understanding. Encourage employees to embrace and celebrate differences.

- Diverse Leadership: Promote diversity in leadership roles to ensure a variety of perspectives and experiences are represented. This can enhance decision-making and innovation.

Ensuring Financial Stability

Financial stability is the cornerstone of a successful and sustainable business. It involves managing cash flow, maintaining healthy profit margins, stocking strong selling products and building reserves for unforeseen challenges.

Cash Flow Management:

- Cash Flow Forecasting: Develop accurate cash flow forecasts to anticipate and plan for future cash needs. Monitor cash flow regularly to identify and address potential issues.

- Receivables Management: Implement effective receivables management practices to ensure timely collection of payments. Offer incentives for early payments and follow up on overdue accounts.

- Expense Control: Monitor and control expenses to maintain a positive cash flow. Identify areas where costs can be reduced without compromising quality or efficiency.

Profit Margin Optimization:

- Pricing Strategy: Develop a pricing strategy that maximizes profit margins while remaining competitive. Consider factors such as cost of goods sold, market demand, and competitor pricing.

- Cost Efficiency: Identify and implement cost-saving measures to improve profit margins. This may include renegotiating supplier contracts, optimizing production processes, and reducing waste.

- Value Proposition: Enhance the company's value proposition to justify premium pricing. Focus on delivering exceptional value and quality to customers.

Building Reserves:

- Emergency Fund: Build an emergency fund to cover unexpected expenses and financial challenges. This fund should be easily accessible and sufficient to cover several months of operating costs.

- Investment Strategy: Develop a sound investment strategy to grow reserves and generate additional income. Consider low-risk investment options that provide stable returns.

- Risk Management: Implement risk management practices to identify and mitigate potential financial risks. This may include diversifying revenue streams, purchasing insurance, and developing contingency plans or exit strategies.

Balance and stability are fundamental principles that underpin success in both martial arts and business. In martial arts, maintaining a balanced stance and stable posture allows practitioners to generate power, move efficiently, and respond effectively to opponents. Similarly, in business, achieving balance and stability involves managing resources wisely to ensure financial stability, fostering a strong organizational culture.

By implementing effective resource management practices, businesses can optimize the use of financial, human, and material resources to support growth and sustainability. Maintaining a strong organizational culture fosters employee engagement, loyalty, and productivity, creating a resilient and adaptable workforce. Ensuring financial stability involves managing cash flow, optimizing profit margins, and building reserves to withstand challenges and seize opportunities. Businesses that prioritize balance and stability are better positioned to achieve long-term success and growth. They can navigate challenges, adapt to change, and capitalize on opportunities while maintaining a solid foundation. Where a martial artist's strength and effectiveness stem from balance and stability, a business's ability to thrive in a dynamic and competitive environment depends on its commitment to these core principles.

14.

Continuous Learning: The Role of Training and Development

In the dynamic world of martial arts, continuous learning and training are fundamental to achieving mastery. Similarly, in the ever-evolving business landscape, the commitment to ongoing development and staying updated with industry trends is essential for sustaining competitive advantage. There are many parallels between the discipline of martial arts and business, and emphasizing the value of investing in employee development. In martial arts you are learning more than how to fight or develop self-discipline, you are also building a community and developing yourself and your students.

Continuous Learning in Martial Arts

Martial arts, encompassing disciplines such as Karate, Judo, Taekwondo, and Brazilian Jiu-Jitsu, require practitioners to engage in lifelong learning. Here are key aspects of continuous learning in martial arts:

Technique Refinement:
Martial artists constantly refine their techniques to improve efficiency and effectiveness. This involves repetition in classes, feedback from instructors, and self-assessment.

Physical and Mental Conditioning:
Continuous training builds physical strength, flexibility, and endurance. Equally important is mental conditioning, which includes developing focus, discipline, and resilience.

Retention of training:
Through the continuous training and repetition of techniques you help to build retention of techniques. The retention of techniques is where you are able to draw on the experiences of training to apply in real world situations.

Learning from Experience:
Martial artists learn from their experiences, both successes and failures. Each bout, whether in training or competition, offers insights that contribute to growth.

The Parallel in Business: Continuous Learning and Employee Development

In the business world, the principles of continuous learning and training are equally vital. Organizations that invest in employee development reap numerous benefits, including enhanced performance, innovation, and adaptability. Key elements include:

Skill Refinement:
Similar to how martial artists refine their techniques, employees must continually upgrade their skills to remain relevant. This includes technical skills, soft skills, and leadership abilities.

Employee Engagement and Retention:
Providing opportunities for growth and development fosters employee engagement and loyalty. Employees who feel valued and supported have higher job satisfaction and are more likely to stay with the company and contribute their best efforts.

Innovation from experience:
A culture of continuous learning encourages innovation. Employees who are up-to-date with industry trends and best practices can contribute fresh ideas that drive the company's competitive edge.

Investing in Employee Development

Investing in employee development is a strategic imperative for organizations aiming to thrive in today's competitive landscape. Here are key strategies for fostering a culture of continuous learning:

Training Programs and Workshops:
Offer regular training programs and workshops that focus on skill development, leadership training, and industry-specific knowledge.

Mentorship and Coaching:
Establish mentorship and coaching programs where experienced employees can guide and support the development of newer or less experienced colleagues.

Access to Resources:
Provide access to learning resources such as online courses,

industry publications, and conferences. Encouraging self-directed learning helps employees stay current with industry trends.

Performance Feedback and Development Plans:
Implement a structured process for providing performance feedback and creating personalized development plans. This helps employees understand their strengths, identify areas for improvement, and set actionable goals.

Encouraging Innovation:
Create an environment where employees feel empowered to experiment and innovate. This can be facilitated through initiatives like brainstorming sessions, innovation labs, and cross-functional projects.

Examples of Companies Prioritizing Learning and Development

Multiple companies have distinguished themselves by making learning and development a core part of their organizational culture. Here are a few notable examples:

1. Microsoft: Microsoft has made significant investments in learning and development through its "Microsoft Learn" platform, which provides employees with access to a wealth of training resources. The company also emphasizes a growth mindset, encouraging employees to embrace challenges and learn from failures. [17]

2. Deloitte: Deloitte's commitment to employee development is evident through its comprehensive learning programs. The company's "Deloitte University" offers leadership and technical training, while its "Greenhouse" innovation labs provide a space for employees to collaborate and experiment with new ideas. [18]

3. Salesforce: Salesforce places a strong emphasis on continuous learning with its "Trailhead" platform, which offers gamified learning experiences. The company also encourages employees to develop new skills through certifications and hands-on projects. [19]

4. IBM: IBM has a long history of prioritizing employee development. The company's "Your Learning" platform provides personalized learning experiences, while its "Think Academy" offers in-depth training on emerging technologies and industry trends. [20]

Benefits of Continuous Learning and Training in Business

The benefits of continuous learning and training in business are manifold. Here are some key advantages:

Enhanced Performance and Productivity:
Employees who are continually learning and developing new skills are more productive and perform at a higher level. This directly contributes to the organization's success.

Increased Employee Engagement:
Investing in employee development shows a commitment to their growth and well-being, leading to higher levels of engagement and job satisfaction.

Greater Innovation:
A culture of continuous learning fosters creativity and innovation. Employees are more likely to come up with new ideas and solutions when they are exposed to the latest trends and technologies.

Adaptability to Change:
Organizations that prioritize learning and development are better equipped to navigate changes in the market and

industry. Employees who are adaptable can help the company pivot and seize new opportunities.

Attraction and Retention of Talent:
Companies that invest in employee development attract top talent. High-potential candidates are drawn to organizations that offer opportunities for growth and advancement.

Implementing Continuous Learning and Development: Best Practices

To effectively implement a culture of continuous learning and development, organizations should consider the following best practices:

Leadership Commitment:
Leadership must demonstrate a commitment to learning and development. This includes allocating resources, setting an example, and communicating the importance of continuous improvement.

Employee Involvement:
Involve employees in the development of learning programs. Seek their input on training needs and preferences to ensure that the programs are relevant and engaging.

Regular Assessment and Feedback:
Continuously assess the effectiveness of learning programs and seek feedback from employees. This helps in refining the programs to ensure they meet the evolving needs of the workforce.

Integration with Career Development:
Align learning and development initiatives with career development plans. This ensures that employees see a clear path for growth and are motivated to participate in training programs.

Leveraging Technology:
Utilize technology to deliver learning experiences. Online learning platforms, virtual classrooms, and mobile apps make it easier for employees to access training materials anytime, anywhere.

The principles of continuous learning and training in martial arts provide valuable insights for the business world. By investing in employee development and staying updated with industry trends, organizations can enhance performance, foster innovation, and maintain a competitive edge. The examples of companies like Microsoft, Deloitte, Salesforce, and IBM illustrate the tangible benefits of prioritizing learning and development. As the business landscape continues to evolve, the commitment to continuous improvement will remain a key driver of success.

15.

Resilience and Recovery: Bouncing Back from Setbacks

Resilience, the ability to withstand adversity and recover from setbacks, is a fundamental trait both in martial arts and in the business world. Whether facing a formidable opponent in the dojo or navigating the complexities of the corporate landscape, resilience enables individuals and organizations to endure challenges, adapt, and ultimately thrive.

Understanding Resilience

Resilience is the capacity to recover quickly from difficulties and adapt to changing circumstances. In martial arts, resilience is essential for mastering techniques, enduring rigorous training, and facing opponents. Similarly, in business, resilience allows companies to navigate market fluctuations, competitive pressures, and internal crises.

Key Components of Resilience:

1. Mental Toughness: The ability to stay focused, remain calm under pressure, continue to visualise your goal and maintain a positive attitude.

2. Adaptability: The capacity to adjust strategies and approaches in response to changing conditions.

3. Perseverance: The determination to continue efforts despite difficulties and setbacks.

4. Learning from Failures: The ability to analyse failures, extract valuable lessons, and apply them to future endeavours.

Resilience in Martial Arts

Martial arts training inherently builds resilience. Practitioners face physical, mental, and emotional challenges that test their limits and require continuous growth.

Physical Resilience

Physical resilience in martial arts involves enduring rigorous training, recovering from injuries, and maintaining peak physical condition. Techniques to build physical resilience include:

1. Consistent Training: Regular practice and conditioning help martial artists build endurance and strength.

2. Injury Prevention and Recovery: Proper warm-ups, stretching, and rest periods are crucial for preventing injuries. When injuries occur, a disciplined recovery process ensures a swift return to training.

3. Nutrition and Hydration: A balanced diet and adequate hydration support overall health and physical resilience.

Mental Resilience

Mental resilience is the ability to stay focused, manage stress, and maintain a positive mindset. Strategies to enhance mental resilience include:

1. Meditation and Mindfulness: Practices such as meditation and mindfulness help martial artists stay present and manage stress.

2. Visualization: Imagining successful techniques and outcomes can boost confidence and prepare practitioners for real-life scenarios.

3. Goal Setting: Setting and achieving short-term and long-term goals keeps martial artists motivated and focused.

Resilience in Business

In the business world, resilience is crucial for navigating uncertainties, financial set-backs, market fluctuations, and internal challenges. Resilient organizations are better equipped to recover from setbacks through adaptation of processes and seize opportunities.

Strategies for Recovering from Setbacks

1. <u>Developing a Crisis Management Plan:</u> A well-defined crisis management plan prepares businesses to respond swiftly and effectively to unexpected challenges. This includes identifying potential risks, assigning roles and responsibilities, and outlining communication strategies.

2. <u>Maintaining Financial Reserves:</u> Building financial reserves ensures that businesses have the resources to weather economic downturns or unexpected expenses. This involves prudent financial planning, budgeting, and maintaining liquidity.

3. <u>Diversifying Revenue Streams:</u> Relying on multiple revenue sources reduces the impact of a downturn in any single area. Businesses can diversify by exploring new markets, expanding product lines, finding new market sectors or developing new services.

Learning from Failures

1. <u>Conducting Post-Mortem Analyses:</u> After a failure, conducting a thorough analysis helps identify the root causes and key lessons. This involves gathering input from all stakeholders, evaluating what went wrong, and developing strategies to avoid similar issues in the future.

2. Encouraging a Growth Mindset: Cultivating a culture that views failures as learning opportunities fosters innovation and continuous improvement. Leaders should encourage experimentation, reward risk-taking, and celebrate lessons learned from failures.

3. Implementing Continuous Improvement Processes: Adopting methodologies such as Lean [21], Six Sigma [22], or Agile [23] encourages ongoing evaluation and refinement of processes. This helps businesses identify inefficiencies, make incremental improvements, and enhance overall performance. These are simple to implement manually if you aren't wanting to add another software to your technology deck. The key parts to focus on are: DMAIC (Define, Measure, Analyze, Improve, Control) these are the problem-solving steps used to improve existing processes by identifying and eliminating the root causes.

Building a Resilient Organization

1. Fostering a Positive Organizational Culture: A positive culture promotes teamwork, trust, and employee engagement. Leaders should prioritize transparency through open communication, and recognition of achievements to build a strong, cohesive team.

2. Investing in Employee Development: Providing training and development opportunities equips employees with the skills and knowledge needed to adapt to change. This includes offering professional development programs and mentoring.

3. Enhancing Operational Flexibility: Building flexibility into operations enables businesses to respond quickly to changing market conditions. This can

involve adopting flexible work arrangements, leveraging technology to streamline processes, and creating adaptable business models.

Stories of Resilient Businesses

Starbucks: Navigating Economic Downturns

In the late 2000s, Starbucks faced significant challenges as the global economic downturn led to declining sales and store closures. However, the company demonstrated resilience by implementing several key strategies:

1. <u>Reevaluating and Refocusing:</u> Starbucks closed underperforming stores and streamlined its menu to focus on core offerings. This helped reduce costs and improve operational efficiency.

2. <u>Innovating and Diversifying:</u> The company introduced new products, such as instant coffee and VIA Ready Brew, to attract cost-conscious consumers. Starbucks also expanded its digital presence and loyalty programs to enhance customer engagement.

3. <u>Emphasizing Corporate Social Responsibility:</u> By prioritizing ethical sourcing, environmental sustainability, and community engagement, Starbucks strengthened its brand reputation and customer loyalty.

Through these efforts, Starbucks not only weathered the economic downturn but emerged stronger, with a renewed focus on growth and innovation.

LEGO: Reinventing a Classic Brand

In the early 2000s, LEGO faced declining sales and financial losses, leading to concerns about the company's future.

However, LEGO's resilience enabled it to turn its fortunes around:

1. Focusing on Core Strengths: LEGO returned to its core product, the iconic brick, and discontinued underperforming product lines. This renewed focus helped streamline operations and improve product quality.

2. Innovating and Expanding: LEGO embraced digital technology by launching video games, movies, and online platforms that complemented its physical products. This attracted a new generation of customers and expanded the brand's reach.

3. Collaborating and Co-Creating: LEGO engaged with its fan community through initiatives like LEGO Ideas, which allowed fans to submit and vote on new product ideas. This fostered a sense of ownership and loyalty among customers.

By embracing innovation and staying true to its core values, LEGO successfully revitalized its brand and achieved sustained growth.

Resilience is a vital quality in both martial arts and business, enabling individuals and organizations to overcome setbacks, adapt to change, and achieve success. By understanding and cultivating resilience, businesses can navigate challenges, learn from failures, and build a foundation for long-term growth and innovation. The stories of Starbucks and LEGO illustrate the power of resilience in transforming challenges into opportunities. Whether in the dojo or the boardroom, resilience is the key to enduring adversity and emerging stronger on the other side. By adopting strategies such as developing crisis management plans, maintaining financial reserves, fostering a positive organizational culture, and encouraging continuous improvement, businesses can build resilience and thrive in an ever-changing world.

16.

Building a Team: Leveraging Collective Strengths

Teamwork is a cornerstone of success in both martial arts and business. In martial arts, a cohesive team can enhance training experiences, improve skill development, and foster a supportive environment. Similarly, in business, strong team dynamics can lead to innovative solutions, higher productivity, and a positive workplace culture.

Teamwork in Martial Arts

The Dojo as a Team Environment
In martial arts, the dojo is more than just a place to train; it is a community where practitioners come together to learn, grow, and support one another. Each member of the dojo contributes to the overall learning experience, creating a dynamic environment where everyone benefits from shared knowledge and experience.

1. <u>Shared Goals and Mutual Support:</u> Martial artists often have individual goals, but they also work towards common objectives, such as preparing for competitions or mastering new techniques. This shared focus fosters a sense of camaraderie and mutual support. Practitioners encourage and challenge each other, creating a positive feedback loop that accelerates progress.
2. <u>Leveraging Individual Strengths:</u> Every martial artist has unique strengths and weaknesses. In a team setting, members can leverage their individual strengths to help others improve. For instance, a practitioner with excellent flexibility can help teammates improve their stretching routines, while someone with strong technical skills can offer insights into refining techniques.
3. <u>Building Trust and Respect:</u> Trust and respect are fundamental in martial arts. Practitioners must trust their partners during sparring sessions and respect each other's boundaries and safety. This trust extends beyond physical interactions, fostering an environment where members feel safe to share their experiences and learn from one another.

Brazilian Jiu-Jitsu (BJJ) Teams

Brazilian Jiu-Jitsu (BJJ) is a martial art that emphasizes ground fighting and submissions. BJJ teams exemplify the importance of teamwork in martial arts. Training partners play a crucial role in each other's development, providing resistance, feedback, and support.

Team Dynamics in BJJ:

1. Collaborative Learning: BJJ practitioners often engage in "rolling" sessions, where they spar with partners of varying skill levels. These sessions are opportunities for learning and improvement, as more experienced practitioners can guide beginners and offer constructive feedback.

2. Community Events: Many BJJ academies host seminars, open mats, and competitions that bring the community together. These events strengthen team bonds and provide additional learning opportunities.

3. Mentorship: Experienced practitioners often take on mentorship roles, helping newer members navigate the complexities of BJJ. This mentorship fosters a culture of continuous learning and mutual support.

Teamwork in Business

Building Strong Teams

In the business world, teamwork is essential for achieving organizational goals and driving innovation. Effective teams leverage the diverse skills and perspectives of their members, creating a collaborative environment where ideas can flourish.

1. <u>Clear Roles and Responsibilities:</u> Defining clear roles and responsibilities ensures that each team member understands their contribution to the team's objectives. This clarity reduces confusion and enhances accountability, allowing the team to function more efficiently.
2. <u>Leveraging Individual Strengths:</u> Recognizing and leveraging individual strengths is as crucial in business as it is in martial arts. Team members with complementary skills can collaborate effectively, filling in gaps and enhancing overall performance. For example, a team might include individuals with expertise in marketing, finance, and product development, each contributing their unique strengths to achieve common goals.
3. <u>Fostering a Collaborative Environment:</u> A collaborative environment encourages open communication, idea sharing, and collective problem-solving. Teams that foster collaboration are more likely to generate innovative solutions and adapt to challenges. This environment is characterized by trust, respect, and a willingness to listen to and value diverse perspectives.

Google's Project Aristotle

Google conducted an extensive study called Project Aristotle to understand what makes a team effective. The study revealed that the most important factor in team success is psychological safety, which is the belief that team members can speak up without fear of ridicule or punishment. [24]

Key Findings from Project Aristotle:

- <u>Psychological Safety:</u> Teams with high psychological safety are more likely to take risks, share ideas, and admit mistakes, leading to greater innovation and problem-solving.

- Dependability: Team members who can rely on each other to meet deadlines and deliver quality work contribute to a stronger, more cohesive team.

- Structure and Clarity: Clear goals, roles, and plans help teams stay focused and aligned with organizational objectives.

- Meaning: When team members find their work personally meaningful, they are more motivated and engaged.

- Impact: Understanding how their work contributes to the organization's success gives team members a sense of purpose and drives performance.

Integrating Martial Arts Principles into Business Teamwork

Businesses can draw valuable lessons from martial arts to build stronger teams. The principles of trust, respect, leveraging individual strengths, and fostering a collaborative environment are directly applicable to the business context.

Building Trust and Respect

In martial arts, trust and respect are foundational. Businesses can cultivate these qualities by encouraging open communication, recognizing contributions, and creating a safe environment for idea exchange.

Strategies for Building Trust and Respect:

- Transparent Communication: Encourage honest and open communication. Leaders should model transparency and create channels for feedback and dialogue.

- Recognition and Appreciation: Regularly acknowledge and celebrate team members' achievements and contributions. This recognition fosters a culture of respect and appreciation.

- Team-Building Activities: Engage in team-building activities that promote trust and collaboration. These activities can range from workshops and retreats to collaborative projects and social events.

Leveraging Individual Strengths

Recognizing and utilizing individual strengths enhances team performance. In martial arts, practitioners learn to leverage their unique abilities to benefit the team. Similarly, businesses can identify and harness the diverse skills of their team members.

Strategies for Leveraging Individual Strengths:

- Strengths Assessment: Conduct assessments to identify team members' strengths and areas of expertise. Tools like StrengthsFinder [25] or Myers-Briggs [26] can provide valuable insights.

- Role Alignment: Align roles and responsibilities with individual strengths. Ensure that team members are placed in positions where they can excel and contribute most effectively.

- Cross-Training: Encourage cross-training and skill development. Allow team members to learn from each other and expand their capabilities, enhancing the overall strength of the team.

Fostering a Collaborative Environment

Collaboration is key to innovation and problem-solving. Martial arts teams thrive on collaboration, learning from each other and working together towards common goals. Businesses can create a similar environment by promoting teamwork and open communication.

Strategies for Fostering Collaboration:

- Collaborative Tools: Implement tools and technologies that facilitate collaboration, such as project management software, communication platforms, and collaborative workspaces.

- Team Projects: Assign projects that require collective effort and collaboration. Encourage team members to work together, share ideas, and solve problems as a unit.

- Open Forums: Create opportunities for open forums and brainstorming sessions. Encourage team members to share their ideas and perspectives, fostering a culture of innovation and creativity.

Companies with Exceptional Team Dynamics

Zappos

Zappos, an online shoe and clothing retailer, is renowned for its exceptional team dynamics and unique company culture. The company places a strong emphasis on employee happiness, collaboration, and customer satisfaction.

Key Aspects of Zappos' Team Dynamics:

- Holacracy: Zappos adopted a holacracy system, which replaces traditional management hierarchies with self-organizing teams. This system empowers employees to take ownership of their roles and collaborate more effectively.

- <u>Core Values:</u> Zappos' core values emphasize teamwork, humility, and embracing change. These values guide the company's culture and influence how teams interact and work together.

- <u>Employee Empowerment:</u> Zappos empowers employees to make decisions and take initiative. This empowerment fosters a sense of ownership and accountability, enhancing team dynamics.

Pixar

Pixar, the renowned animation studio, is another example of a company with exceptional team dynamics. Pixar's collaborative environment and creative culture have produced numerous successful films.

Key Aspects of Pixar's Team Dynamics:

- <u>Braintrust Meetings</u>: Pixar's Braintrust meetings involve a group of experienced directors and storytellers who provide candid feedback on projects. These meetings encourage open dialogue and constructive criticism, leading to better outcomes.

- <u>Creative Collaboration:</u> Pixar fosters a culture of creative collaboration, where team members from different departments work together to bring stories to life. This collaboration leverages diverse skills and perspectives, resulting in innovative films.

- <u>Supportive Culture:</u> Pixar promotes a supportive culture where team members feel valued and respected. This culture encourages risk-taking and experimentation, essential for creative success.

Patagonia

Patagonia, an outdoor clothing and gear company, is known for its commitment to environmental sustainability and strong team dynamics. The company's values-driven approach influences how teams operate and collaborate.

Key Aspects of Patagonia's Team Dynamics:

- <u>Mission-Driven Culture:</u> Patagonia's mission to "save our home planet" unites employees around a common goal. This shared purpose fosters a sense of camaraderie and collaboration.

- <u>Empowerment and Trust:</u> Patagonia empowers employees to take initiative and make decisions aligned with the company's values. This trust in employees enhances team dynamics and accountability.

- <u>Inclusive Environment:</u> Patagonia promotes an inclusive environment where diverse voices are heard and valued. This inclusivity strengthens team dynamics and fosters innovation.

Teamwork is a vital element in both martial arts and business. In martial arts, a cohesive team enhances training experiences, skill development, and mutual support. In business, strong team dynamics drive innovation, productivity, and a positive workplace culture. By building trust, respect, and leveraging individual strengths, you can cultivate a business that thrives on collaboration, adapts to challenges, and consistently outperforms competitors. A well-integrated team not only boosts overall efficiency but also fosters creativity and resilience, positioning the business for long-term success and sustainable growth.

17.

The Power of Perception and Reputation: Shaping Your Image

Perception is a critical factor that shapes the outcomes in both martial arts and business. In martial arts, perception determines how an opponent's movements and intentions are interpreted, guiding strategic responses. Similarly, in business, perception influences how a company is viewed by its customers, stakeholders, and competitors, affecting its reputation and success. It is important to understand how the power and role of perception is shaping your image, there are many strategies for shaping and managing images and brand reputation. Having a strong brand image and purpose is key for any company as it is the one thing that can pull a business together or create disputes and pull a company apart.

The Role of Perception in Martial Arts

In martial arts, perception is about more than just physical sight. It encompasses awareness, intuition, and the ability to read an opponent's intentions and actions. A martial artist's success often hinges on their ability to perceive subtle cues and react accordingly. This heightened sense of perception allows martial artists to anticipate moves, counter attacks, and exploit weaknesses.

Key Aspects of Perception in Martial Arts

1. Awareness: Martial artists must maintain a high level of situational awareness. This means being attuned to their surroundings, understanding the dynamics of a fight, and staying focused on the present moment. Awareness helps in anticipating the opponent's moves and reacting swiftly.

2. Reading Opponents: Successful martial artists are adept at reading their opponents. They observe body language, eye movements, and breathing patterns to gauge the opponent's intentions. This ability to read

subtle cues can provide a significant advantage in combat.

3. <u>Adaptability:</u> Perception in martial arts also involves being adaptable. A martial artist must adjust their strategy based on the opponent's actions and the changing dynamics of a fight. This flexibility is crucial for success in unpredictable situations.

4. <u>Timing and Distance:</u> Effective perception involves understanding the concepts of timing and distance. Knowing when to strike and maintaining the appropriate distance can make the difference between victory and defeat.

5. <u>Aura:</u> High level martial artists seem to have a certain aura about them where you can sense that they know how to protect themselves and fight. This may unconsciously be in how they hold themselves, how they communicate confidently or how they are not afraid to make eye contact. This aura can be used to stop conflict prior to it starting or it can be used to help influence the room. To do this you can put your body into a position such as crossed arms, then wait for others to cross their arms. You can then change your position and see if the others move into the same position such as leaning against a table. If they do then your posture and body language is controlling the room meaning you can control the flow of conversation with your body cues. [27]

The Role of Perception and Reputation in Business

In the business world, perception plays a similar role. A company's success is heavily influenced by how it is perceived by customers, investors, employees, and the public. Positive perception can lead to increased sales, customer loyalty, and a strong brand reputation, while negative perception can result in loss of business and credibility.

Key Aspects of Perception and Reputation in Business

1. Brand Image: A company's brand image is how it is perceived in the marketplace. It encompasses the company's values, mission, and the quality of its products or services. A strong brand image attracts customers and builds trust.

2. Reputation Management: Managing a company's reputation involves actively shaping and maintaining a positive image. This includes handling public relations, responding to customer feedback, and addressing any negative publicity promptly and effectively.

3. Customer Perception: Understanding and influencing customer perception is vital for business success. Companies must ensure that their marketing messages align with customer expectations and needs.

4. Stakeholder Perception: Companies must also manage the perception of stakeholders, including investors, employees, and partners. A positive perception among stakeholders can lead to increased investment, employee satisfaction, and beneficial partnerships.

Strategies for Shaping and Managing Business Perception

To effectively shape and manage perception, businesses can employ several strategies. These strategies focus on building a strong brand image, maintaining a positive reputation, and influencing customer and stakeholder perceptions.

Building a Strong Brand Image

A strong brand image is built on a foundation of consistent messaging, high-quality products or services, and a clear value proposition.

Consistent Messaging: Ensure that all communications, from marketing materials to customer service interactions, convey a consistent message. This helps reinforce the brand's values and promises.

Quality Products and Services: Delivering high-quality products and services is crucial for building a positive brand image. Consistently meeting or exceeding customer expectations fosters trust and loyalty.

Clear Value Proposition: A clear and compelling value proposition sets a brand apart from its competitors. It communicates the unique benefits that customers can expect from the brand.

Reputation Management

Effective reputation management involves monitoring public perception, addressing negative feedback, and engaging in proactive public relations efforts.

Monitoring Public Perception: Regularly monitor social media, review sites, and other platforms to understand how the brand is perceived. This helps identify potential issues early and address them promptly.

Addressing Negative Feedback: Respond to negative feedback professionally and constructively. Apologize when necessary, and take steps to resolve the issue. This shows customers that the company values their feedback and is committed to improvement.

Proactive Public Relations: Engage in proactive public relations efforts to shape positive perception. This can include press releases, media interviews, community engagement, and corporate social responsibility initiatives.

Influencing Customer Perception

Influencing customer perception involves understanding customer needs, delivering value, and creating positive experiences.

Understanding Customer Needs: Conduct market research to understand customer needs and preferences. Use this information to tailor products, services, and marketing messages.

Delivering Value: Ensure that the products or services deliver real value to customers. This includes meeting functional needs, providing excellent customer service, and creating memorable experiences.

Creating Positive Experiences: Focus on creating positive customer experiences at every touchpoint. This includes user-friendly websites, responsive customer support, and personalized interactions.

Managing Stakeholder Perception

Managing stakeholder perception involves transparent communication, delivering on promises, and building strong relationships.

Transparent Communication: Maintain open and honest communication with stakeholders. This builds trust and fosters positive relationships.

Delivering on Promises: Ensure that the company delivers on its promises to stakeholders, whether it's financial performance for investors or career development opportunities for employees.

Building Strong Relationships: Invest in building strong relationships with stakeholders. This can include regular updates, engaging in dialogue, and addressing concerns promptly.

Successful Branding and Public Relations Campaigns

Successful branding and public relations campaigns can significantly influence perception and enhance a company's image and reputation. Here are a few notable examples:

Dove's "Real Beauty" Campaign

Dove's "Real Beauty" campaign aimed to challenge traditional beauty standards and promote body positivity. The campaign featured real women of diverse shapes, sizes, and ages, celebrating their natural beauty. Dove's message resonated with consumers and sparked a broader conversation about beauty standards, significantly enhancing the brand's image. [28]

Coca-Cola's "Share a Coke" Campaign

Coca-Cola's "Share a Coke" campaign involved replacing the iconic Coca-Cola logo on bottles with popular names. The campaign encouraged consumers to find bottles with their names or the names of their friends and family, fostering a sense of personalization and connection. The campaign was a massive success, boosting sales and engagement. [29]

Nike's "Just Do It" Campaign

Nike's "Just Do It" campaign is one of the most iconic branding campaigns in history. Launched in 1988, the campaign featured inspiring athletes and emphasized the idea that anyone could achieve greatness through determination and effort. The campaign's powerful message and emotional appeal solidified Nike's brand identity and positioned it as a leader in the sports industry. [30]

Perception plays a crucial role in both martial arts and business. To shape and manage perception effectively, businesses must focus on building a strong brand image, managing their reputation, influencing customer perception, and managing stakeholder relationships. By employing strategies such as consistent messaging, delivering quality products, proactive public relations, and transparent communication, companies can create a positive perception and enhance their brand reputation.

Successful branding and public relations campaigns, like Dove's "Real Beauty," Coca-Cola's "Share a Coke," and Nike's "Just Do It," demonstrate the power of perception in shaping a company's image and reputation. These campaigns highlight the importance of understanding and influencing perception to achieve business success.

The power of perception cannot be underestimated in martial arts and business. By honing their ability to perceive and influence, practitioners and companies alike can navigate challenges, seize opportunities, and achieve lasting success.

18.

Ethical Strategy: Winning with Integrity

The principles of ethics and integrity are foundational to achieving long-term success and maintaining a positive reputation. Martial arts, with its roots in ancient traditions and philosophies, emphasizes moral conduct, respect, and discipline. Similarly, businesses that prioritize ethical principles often see sustained growth, customer loyalty, and respect within their industry. The importance of ethics and integrity in martial arts and business is key in this climate, together we will illustrate how these principles can be applied to achieve success without compromising moral values. We will also delve into case studies of companies that have upheld integrity in their business practices.

Ethics and Integrity in Martial Arts

The Philosophical Foundations
Martial arts are not merely physical practices but also embody rich philosophical traditions. Many martial arts styles, such as Karate, Judo, and Taekwondo, emphasize the development of character alongside physical skills. The teachings often focus on respect for others, humility, and the importance of living a life of integrity.

1. Respect and Humility: Martial arts training begins and ends with a bow, a gesture of respect to the instructor, the training partners, and the art itself. This practice instils a deep sense of humility and reminds practitioners of the importance of respect in all interactions.

2. Discipline and Self-Control: Martial artists are trained to control their impulses and respond to situations with calmness and thoughtfulness. This discipline extends beyond the dojo, influencing how they conduct themselves in daily life.

3. Honesty and Integrity: The concept of 'the way' in martial arts refers to a path of honesty and integrity. Practitioners are encouraged to be truthful in their dealings and to maintain high ethical standards.

Practical Applications in Training
In martial arts, integrity manifests in various ways, including fair play, honest self-assessment, and adherence to rules and traditions. Practitioners are taught to win with honour and lose with dignity, emphasizing the value of effort and personal growth over victory.

1. Fair Play: Sparring and competitions in martial arts are governed by strict rules to ensure fairness. Practitioners learn to compete honourably, without resorting to deceit or unsportsmanlike behaviour.

2. Honest Self-Assessment: Martial artists are encouraged to continuously assess their abilities and progress honestly. This self-reflection fosters a growth mindset and helps practitioners strive for constant improvement.

3. Adherence to Tradition: Respecting the traditions and teachings of martial arts is a critical aspect of maintaining the integrity of the practice. This respect for the past helps preserve the art for future generations.

Ethics and Integrity in Business

The Role of Ethical Principles

In the business world, ethics and integrity are equally important. Companies that prioritize ethical behaviour build trust with their customers, employees, and stakeholders. Ethical business practices lead to a positive reputation, legal compliance, and a strong corporate culture.

1. Building Trust: Trust is the cornerstone of any successful business relationship. Companies that consistently demonstrate integrity earn the trust of their customers and partners, leading to long-term loyalty and collaboration.

2. Positive Reputation: A reputation for ethical behaviour attracts customers, investors, and top talent. Companies known for their integrity are often seen as leaders in their industry.

3. Legal Compliance: Adhering to ethical standards helps businesses avoid legal issues and the associated costs and reputational damage. Compliance with laws and regulations is a fundamental aspect of ethical business practices.

4. Strong Corporate Culture: Companies that prioritize ethics create a positive work environment. Employees are more likely to feel valued and motivated, leading to higher productivity and job satisfaction.

Strategies for Maintaining Integrity
To maintain integrity, businesses must implement strategies that promote ethical behaviour at all levels of the organization. This includes establishing a clear code of conduct, providing ethics training, and fostering an open and transparent culture.

1. Code of Conduct: A well-defined code of conduct outlines the ethical standards and expectations for all employees. This document serves as a guide for decision-making and helps prevent unethical behaviour.

2. Ethics Training: Regular training programs ensure that employees understand the importance of ethics and how to apply ethical principles in their daily work. Training should cover topics such as conflict of interest, anti-corruption, and respectful workplace behaviour.

3. Transparent Culture: Encouraging open communication and transparency helps identify and address ethical issues before they escalate. An environment where employees feel comfortable

reporting concerns without fear of retaliation is crucial.

4. Leadership by Example: Leaders play a critical role in setting the tone for ethical behaviour. When leaders demonstrate integrity, it sets a standard for the entire organization.

Patagonia: Leading by Example in Environmental Stewardship

Patagonia, which is known for its commitment to environmental sustainability and ethical business practices has built its brand on the principles of reducing environmental impact and promoting social responsibility.

1. Environmental Responsibility: Patagonia has implemented numerous initiatives to minimize its environmental footprint, such as using recycled materials, supporting grassroots environmental organizations, and promoting sustainable agriculture. The company's mission statement, "We're in business to save our home planet," reflects its dedication to environmental ethics. [31]

2. Transparent Supply Chain: Patagonia is committed to transparency in its supply chain. The company provides detailed information about the sourcing and production of its products, ensuring that customers are aware of the environmental and social impact of their purchases. [32]

3. Corporate Activism: Patagonia is known for its corporate activism, taking a stand on various environmental issues. The company has engaged in legal battles to protect public lands and launched campaigns to raise awareness about climate change. [33]

The Body Shop: Pioneering Ethical Consumerism

The Body Shop, a global beauty and cosmetics brand, has long been a pioneer in promoting ethical consumerism. Founded by Anita Roddick in 1976, the company has consistently championed social and environmental causes.

1. <u>Against Animal Testing:</u> The Body Shop was one of the first major cosmetics companies to campaign against animal testing. The company has continued to advocate for cruelty-free products and has influenced industry-wide changes. [34]

2. <u>Fair Trade Practices:</u> The Body Shop sources many of its ingredients through fair trade partnerships, ensuring that producers receive fair wages and work under safe conditions. This commitment to fair trade supports sustainable development and reduces poverty in supplier communities. [35]

3. <u>Social Activism:</u> The Body Shop has launched numerous campaigns addressing social issues such as human trafficking, domestic violence, and women's rights. The company's activism aligns with its ethical values and resonates with socially conscious consumers. [36]

TOMS: Integrating Social Good into Business

TOMS, a footwear and accessories company, is known for its innovative "One for One" business model, which integrates social good into its core operations. For every product sold, TOMS donates a product or service to someone in need.

1. <u>One for One Model:</u> TOMS' business model has provided millions of shoes, glasses, and clean water to people in need around the world. This approach has made a significant impact on global poverty and health. [37]

2. <u>Sustainable Practices:</u> In addition to its philanthropic efforts, TOMS is committed to sustainability. The company uses environmentally friendly materials and processes, striving to reduce its ecological footprint. [38]

3. <u>Corporate Responsibility:</u> TOMS promotes corporate responsibility by encouraging other businesses to adopt similar models of social entrepreneurship. The company's success demonstrates that businesses can thrive while making a positive impact on society. [39]

Unilever: Integrating Sustainability into Business Strategy
Unilever, a global consumer goods company, has made sustainability a central part of its business strategy. The company's Sustainable Living Plan aims to decouple growth from environmental impact and increase positive social impact.

1. <u>Sustainable Sourcing:</u> Unilever is committed to sourcing all its agricultural raw materials sustainably. This includes working with suppliers to improve farming practices and ensure fair labour conditions. [40]

2. <u>Reducing Environmental Impact</u>: Unilever has set ambitious targets to reduce greenhouse gas emissions, water use, and waste across its operations. The company regularly reports on its progress, demonstrating transparency and accountability. [41]

3. <u>Enhancing Livelihoods</u>: Unilever's initiatives to enhance livelihoods include improving health and well-being for millions of people, promoting diversity and inclusion, and supporting smallholder farmers.

These efforts contribute to positive social change and sustainable development. [42]

IKEA: Upholding Ethical Standards in Global Operations
IKEA, the multinational furniture retailer, has committed to maintaining high ethical standards in its global operations. The company's Code of Conduct, known as the "IKEA Way," outlines its commitment to sustainability, social responsibility, and ethical business practices.

1. Sustainable Products: IKEA focuses on designing products that are both affordable and sustainable. This includes using renewable materials, reducing waste, and promoting energy efficiency. [43]

2. Fair Labor Practices: IKEA is dedicated to ensuring fair labour practices throughout its supply chain. The company works with suppliers to improve working conditions, prevent child labour, and promote fair wages. [44]

3. Community Engagement: IKEA engages in various community initiatives, such as supporting refugee programs, promoting children's education, and contributing to disaster relief efforts. These activities align with the company's values and enhance its social impact. [45]

The principles of ethics and integrity are essential for success in both martial arts and business. In martial arts, these values are ingrained in the practice, fostering respect, humility, and discipline. In the business world, ethical behaviour builds trust, enhances reputation, and creates a positive corporate culture.

Businesses can achieve success while adhering to ethical principles by implementing strategies such as establishing a code of conduct, providing ethics training, fostering transparency, and leading by example. The case studies of Patagonia, The Body Shop, TOMS, Unilever, and IKEA demonstrate that maintaining integrity in business practices leads to long-term success and positive social impact.

In an increasingly interconnected and transparent world, the importance of ethics and integrity cannot be overstated. Companies that prioritize these values not only contribute to a better society but also position themselves for sustainable growth and success.

Just as martial artists strive to embody the highest standards of conduct, businesses must commit to ethical principles to navigate the challenges of the modern marketplace.

19.

**Fluidity and Flow:
Use Their Strength to Your
Advantage**

In business as in martial arts life is not rigid, you can't plan for an exact set of circumstances to happen, you have to be fluid. Your strategies need to have a margin of error that allows you to fill the void with a different counter attack that will still help you progress towards your goal. This is where sabaki comes in.

The fluidity of Sabaki

If you stayed rigid against your competitor then you are just both striking away at the same thing waiting for either party to give way and fall. With the introduction of sabaki, your opponent strikes expecting you to counter with an obvious counter attack, you instead move around your opponent to their blind spot and strike as hard as you can to finish the fight in one or two moves maximum.

Practical uses of Sabaki

In business an example could be that you have entered into a price war and it's now a race to the bottom, your opponent is larger than you so it's a losing strategy from your side.

How you would use sabaki in this situation is to:

1. Find what is most important to the opponent such as a key product or a service that only they offer; this is their centre of gravity; this is the part that keeps their whole business standing.
2. Now you knock it off balance. Here you can focus on your differentiating factors to the market leader such as if you are selling tea and your brand has more leaves compared to their tea which contains a higher concentration of twigs which don't offer the depth of flavour.
3. You then attack them direct through their distribution network, you start approaching and on boarding their key clients or people that are unhappy with their products or services.
4. Then throw the finishing strike when they are injured and off balance you could create a final campaign that puts doubt in the end user's mind that the competitor product actually works as well as it should compared to your product. By doing this the

competitor then has to spend massive amounts of energy to try build themselves back up which gives you the opportunity to target all of their other more profitable areas so that when they build back up, they aren't as strong.

Remaining fluid through turmoil

In martial arts students remain fluid leading into a fight by doing exercises such as skipping, pad work or conditioning training to ensure their body is warm and supple enough to throw the techniques that the fight may require. Businesses require the same during times of turmoil, the key parts to focus on are advisor feedback, study of strategies and staying in the trenches.

Advisor feedback:

- You hire advisors for one key thing, advice. The benefit of having advisors supporting you is that they offer a different perspective and usually have experience guiding people through similar situations
- When you are in turmoil and everything is upside down things can seem overwhelming, with advisors being one step removed they will be able to see the situation more clearly as business owners in stuck in the middle of the stress struggle to often see the larger picture and are tending to focus on the immediate issues at hand.
- By focusing on the larger picture and having the support network to guide you through the situation you will be more prepared and you will be able to start thinking creatively again to see new openings or new spaces to attack to ease pressure on your current pain points

Study of strategies:

- Fluidity is helped by a deep understanding of your strategies and the potential outcomes that each move may cause.
- Similar to chess, if you study each individual move you will be able to predict the opponents only options, luckily most corporations tend to follow similar strategies for attacking opponents. They tend to focus initially on tying customers in with long term contracts in exchange for rebates based on ordering which is good for them as it locks out any competition for that client or product. A lot of the time if you pre-empt this you can either jump in and do the same or you can persuade the client that a long-term contract is negative for them as if they don't meet their order requirement usually the corporate will force delivery of the balance of goods each year which will cause cashflow issues for them and thus make life a lot more difficult. That rebuttal usually works.

Staying in the trenches:

- Although it is vital to see the bigger picture so that you can create appropriate strategies to counter your opponents' manoeuvres, you also need to stay with a hand in the trenches to get immediate feedback from the ground level about what is happening.
- Through knowing what is going on at ground level you can see how well your opponents' strategies are landing and what you need to do to adjust your own strategies to defeat them
- Make sure however, that you don't spend too much time in the trenches. It is very easy when you are in the trenches to remain there as you get those dopamine hits of the small wins to keep you going

along with the feeling of camaraderie of being surrounded by your team all fighting together. Although fighting together is important for team spirit, if you are too focused on the trenches then you lose focus of the larger picture. You can never be in two places at once which is why it is important to only keep a hand on the ground, you have team members to report back to you and if you trust them then your line of communication will be strong. This will enable you to make accurate decisions.
- By having a good understanding of what is happening in the trenches through a strong line of communication you can use direct market feedback to guide the flow of your strategies to help you win your war.

Remaining fluid through strong times

As important as remaining fluid through turmoil is, it is just as important in times of strength as a lack of fluidity can lead to stagnation, poor performance a lack of innovation and risk of falling prey to the centre of gravity strategy.

Business stagnation:
When you stay too hard and fast in your current model or strategy then your business can stagnate. This can be caused by staff members that are too 'comfortable' and don't want to progress or improve their own career which means that the driving force behind your company can begin to dissipate.

Poor performance:
When a company consistently misses its targets, poor performance can lead to a sense of complacency and even sadness. It starts to feel normal rather than being recognized as a problem. That's why accurate forecasting and realistic

budgeting are crucial. If your budgets are set too high and seem unattainable, your team may lose motivation, thinking, "Why even bother? We'll never reach the goal anyway." This mindset can be detrimental to your business. If your sales team isn't driven to achieve, they may not be the right fit. You need a team of ambitious, creative, and motivated individuals who will go the extra mile for your clients and themselves, earning commissions or bonuses in return. Always prioritize building a high-performing team that actively tracks and strives to meet their KPIs.

Lack of innovation:
Innovation is essential for continued business growth, just as it is in martial arts. Without innovation, martial arts wouldn't have evolved into the diverse range of styles and techniques we see today, making it less relevant over time. For example, ancient martial arts like Pankration— which combined kicks, wrestling, punches, and joint holds—laid the foundation for modern Mixed Martial Arts (MMA). Although Pankration was effective in its time, it would struggle to compete with today's MMA, where innovations like Brazilian Jiu-Jitsu's ground techniques and the striking arts of Muay Thai and Karate have broadened the strategic landscape for fighters. Similarly, in business, failing to innovate means falling behind. Companies are always seeking new, creative opportunities, so it's critical to explore products or services that have significant market potential and a unique niche to stay competitive.

Fluidity in both martial arts and business is essential for staying adaptable and resilient. The principles of sabaki remind us that rigidly sticking to one strategy can lead to failure. Instead, by staying flexible and responsive, we can handle challenges more effectively. Whether it's through leveraging feedback from advisors, deeply understanding strategic shifts, or maintaining a balance between high-level vision and detailed execution, fluidity ensures we remain ahead of the curve.

In tough times, fluidity helps us adapt and uncover new opportunities. In times of strength, it prevents complacency, driving innovation and continuous improvement. Just as a martial artist must be ready for any move an opponent makes, businesses need to be prepared to pivot and adjust to changing market conditions.

By embracing fluidity and flow, we can turn challenges into opportunities, paving the way for long-term success and growth. The most successful businesses, like the most skilled martial artists, are those that move with precision and adaptability, always ready to seize the right moment.

20.

Conclusion:
The Sabaki Way in Business and Beyond

In martial arts, the sabaki method stands out as a highly strategic approach that emphasizes agility, anticipation, and adaptability. Originating in karate under Hideyuki Ashihara, sabaki teaches the art of moving efficiently to gain control over an opponent and the situation. While deeply rooted in physical combat, this concept extends beyond martial arts and offers valuable insights into business strategy. By examining the principles of sabaki, we uncovered lessons that help to navigate the complexities of the business world more effectively.

At its core, sabaki is about redirecting force, positioning optimally, and mastering precise timing. These principles, though crucial in martial arts, translate seamlessly into the business arena. The ability to anticipate market shifts, adapt swiftly, and strategically position a company can be the difference between success and failure. Just as a martial artist redirects an opponent's force to their advantage, businesses can turn challenges into opportunities. Whether facing market downturns, disruptive competitors, or internal struggles, the sabaki method teaches companies to pivot, innovate, and find new pathways to success.

Positioning is equally important. In Ashihara Karate, it involves moving to an advantageous spot that allows control over the opponent. In business, optimal positioning means finding a market space that leverages a company's strengths and mitigates its weaknesses, ensuring long-term competitive advantage. Timing is also critical, and the ability to make the right move at the right moment can lead to significant gains. This involves a deep understanding of market trends, customer needs, and the competitive landscape, enabling companies to act when opportunities arise.

Beyond specific strategies, sabaki promotes a mindset of agility and adaptability. In today's rapidly changing business environment, companies must pivot quickly and adapt to new conditions. Cultivating this mindset encourages innovation, continuous learning, and resilience. Anticipation plays a key role as well. Just as martial artists anticipate their opponent's next move, businesses must forecast market trends and act proactively rather than reactively. Those that anticipate changes and prepare for them are better positioned to thrive.

These principles of the sabaki method not only apply to business strategy but also enhance personal and professional growth. By embracing agility, adaptability, and strategic thinking, individuals can improve their decision-making and problem-solving skills, better navigating life's challenges. Like martial artists who continuously refine their techniques, professionals should constantly seek opportunities to expand their knowledge and skills to remain competitive and relevant. In professional settings, leaders who foster a culture of agility and adaptability inspire their teams to think creatively and respond effectively to changes and challenges.

Exploring the intersection of martial arts and business offers a rich opportunity for fresh thinking and innovation. By studying sabaki and other martial arts techniques, business professionals can gain new perspectives and strategies for overcoming complex problems. Engaging in martial arts practice itself provides firsthand experience of these principles, enhancing focus, resilience, and strategic thinking. For those interested in deeper exploration, continuing education through workshops and seminars that combine martial arts philosophies with business strategy, such as those offered by Florir Limited (NZ), can provide valuable insights and practical applications.

Ultimately, the sabaki method offers powerful lessons for modern business strategy. By embracing principles such as redirecting force, optimal positioning, precise timing, agility, adaptability, and anticipation, businesses can navigate the ever-changing market landscape more successfully. Encouraging the exploration of martial arts principles in both professional and personal contexts not only leads to a deeper understanding of these strategies but also opens up new avenues for innovation and growth. As we continue to explore the intersection of martial arts and business, we unlock exciting possibilities that foster a more dynamic and resilient approach to today's business challenges.

About the author

John Roberts is a New Zealand born businessman, martial artist and investor; he has a portfolio with a value in the multimillions with businesses and investments in multiple industries. His educational background is in International Trade and Business Strategy.

He has been involved with martial arts since the age of 10 and has achieved a second-dan black belt in Ashihara Karate, trained in other karate styles along with Muay Thai, is currently studying Brazilian Jiu Jitsu under Sorriso/Alliance Jiu Jitsu and is also a Co-Founder of the Kaika Suru Karate Organisation that is designed to continue modernising karate.

John is a family man with a wife: Courtney, and 2 sons: Liam and Ollie. They are his key driving force in life and are how he has been able to achieve his successes.

For further info on the author you can see it on www.florircaptal.com

References

[1] https://www.martialartsprofessional.com/tony-robbins-personal-development-expert-2/

[2] https://www.ashiharakaratesg.com/ashihara-hideyuki.html#:~:text=In%201966%2C%20Ashihara%20was%20given,the%20incident%20attracted%20police%20attention.

[3] https://world.ashihara-karate.net/en/

[4] https://www.britannica.com/biography/Takeda-Shingen

[5] https://www.nytimes.com/2018/04/04/us/politics/cambridge-analytica-scandal-fallout.html

[6] https://www.ou.edu/deptcomm/dodjcc/groups/02C2/Johnson%20&%20Johnson.htm

[7] https://petwineawards.com/

[8] https://www.blueoceanstrategy.com/what-is-blue-ocean-strategy/

[9] https://www.nytimes.com/2020/10/08/technology/ibm-cloud-spinoff.html

[10] https://www.toyota-europe.com/about-us/toyota-vision-and-philosophy/toyota-production-system

[11] https://us.pg.com/blogs/100-years-of-pg-analytics-and-insights/

[12] https://news.airbnb.com/enjoy-the-magic-of-airbnb-experiences-from-the-comfort-of-your-home/

[13] https://www.britannica.com/money/Standard-Oil

[14] https://4birminghamuk.blogspot.com/2012/04/cadbury.html

[15] https://www.snackhistory.com/crunchie/

[16] Fry's Chocolate Dream: The Rise and Fall of a Chocolate Empire – written by Mr John Bradley.

[17] https://learn.microsoft.com/en-us/training/

[18] https://www2.deloitte.com/us/en/pages/about-deloitte/articles/deloitteuniversity-leadership-center.html

[19] https://trailhead.salesforce.com/

[20] https://www.ibm.com/docs/en/your-learning?topic=your-learning-reference-manual

[21] https://www.lean.org/explore-lean/what-is-lean/

[22] https://www.investopedia.com/terms/s/six-sigma.asp

[23] https://www.atlassian.com/agile

[24] https://psychsafety.co.uk/googles-project-aristotle/

[25] https://www.gallup.com/cliftonstrengths/en/254033/strengthsfinder.aspx

[26] https://www.myersbriggs.org/my-mbti-personality-type/myers-briggs-overview/

[27] https://www.forbes.com/sites/work-in-progress/2014/11/17/body-language-rules-to-help-you-command-a-room/

[28] https://www.dove.com/nz/stories/campaigns/real-beauty-pledge.html

[29] https://thebrandhopper.com/2023/06/09/branding-case-study-success-of-share-a-coke-campaign/

[30] https://worldbrandaffairs.com/how-nikes-just-do-it-campaign-became-a-global-phenomenon/

[31] https://www.patagonia.com/our-responsibility-programs.html

[32] https://www.patagonia.com/our-footprint/supply-chain-environmental-responsibility-program.html

[33] https://www.patagonia.com/activism/

[34] https://www.thebodyshop.com/en-gb/about-us/activism/faat/a/a00018

[35] https://www.thebodyshop.com/en-gb/about-us/brand-values/community-fair-trade/a/a00009

[36] https://www.thebodyshop.com/en-gb/about-us/activism/a/a00015

[37] https://www.toms.com/us/about-toms.html

[38] https://www.toms.com/us/impact/planet.html

[39] https://www.toms.com/us/impact.html

[40] https://www.unilever.com/sustainability/nature/sustainable-and-regenerative-sourcing/

[41] https://www.unilever.com/sustainability/safety-and-environment/reducing-our-environmental-impact/

[42] https://www.unilever.com/sustainability/livelihoods/

[43] https://www.ikea.com/gb/en/this-is-ikea/sustainable-everyday/

[44] https://www.ikea.com/global/en/our-business/people-planet/fair-and-equal/

[45] https://www.ikea.com/nz/en/this-is-ikea/community-engagement/

www.ingramcontent.com/pod-product-compliance
Lightning Source LLC
Chambersburg PA
CBHW020657220526
45464CB00001B/466